THE

FATHER

FACTOR

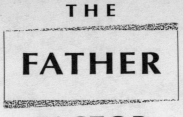

Authors Dr. Henry Biller and Robert Trotter have based their practical advice on the latest and most respected research available. The following is just a sample of some of the areas you will find covered in THE FATHER FACTOR:

- **The decision to have a baby**—Have you considered the effect a baby will have on your wife's educational and career goals? Or on your sense of freedom?
- **Pregnancy**—Don't be a spectator! Your wife will go through enormous changes, but she'll still look to you for emotional and physical affection.
- **The new arrival**—Consider paternity leave, as your presence at home will help establish new family routines, and help you to bond with your newborn.
- **Budding geniuses**—Remember, you are their first teacher. Two fully involved parents gives your child an immeasurable head start on the world of learning.
- **Sons and daughters**—You'll be a different father to girls and to boys, and you will affect their intellectual, moral, and social development in various ways. Your daughter may eventually use you as a yardstick to measure other men; the bond between you and your son is likely to be passed on to his children.

D0423977

THE

FATHER

FACTOR

What You Need to Know to Make a Difference

Henry B. Biller, Ph.D.

AND

Robert J. Trotter

POCKET BOOKS

New York   London   Toronto   Sydney   Tokyo   Singapore

The sale of this book without its cover is unauthorized. If you purchased this book without a cover, you should be aware that it was reported to the publisher as "unsold and destroyed." Neither the author nor the publisher has received payment for the sale of this "stripped book."

An *Original* Publication of POCKET BOOKS

POCKET BOOKS, a division of Simon & Schuster Inc.
1230 Avenue of the Americas, New York, NY 10020

Copyright © 1994 by Henry B. Biller, Ph.D. and Robert J. Trotter

All rights reserved, including the right to reproduce
this book or portions thereof in any form whatsoever.
For information address Pocket Books, 1230 Avenue
of the Americas, New York, NY 10020

Biller, Henry B.
    The father factor : what you need to know to make a difference /
Henry B. Biller and Robert J. Trotter.
        p.   cm.
    Includes bibliographical references and index.
    ISBN 0-671-79397-7
        1. Fatherhood—United States.   2. Father and child—United States.
3. Parenting—United States.   I. Trotter, Robert J.   II. Title.
HQ756.B53   1994
306.874'2—dc20   93-38384
                                                            CIP

First Pocket Books trade paperback printing July 1994

10 9 8 7 6 5 4 3 2 1

POCKET and colophon are registered trademarks of
Simon & Schuster Inc.

Cover design by Tom McKeveny

Cover photo by Telegraph Colour Library/FPG

DESIGN: Stanley S. Drate/Folio Graphics Co. Inc.

Printed in the U.S.A.

To our families, especially our fathers

ACKNOWLEDGMENTS

We thank the hundreds of families who participated in Henry's research projects and who consulted him professionally. Their experiences contributed greatly to this book. We also thank our mutual friend, Dennis Meredith, who suggested that we work together; our agent, Kris Dahl, and her assistant, Dorothea Herrey, at ICM; and our editor, Claire Zion, and Angela Kyle and Michael Sanders at Pocket Books. Finally, we thank Linda Haskell for her helpful comments, Holly Hall for research assistance, Ben and Joe for inspiration, and Margery Salter and Deanna Dunworth for their patience and support.

Contents

Self-Confidence, Morality, and Discipline 115

7

Schooling the Mind and Body 143

Teens and Sexuality 173

Contents

Single, Part-Time, Step-, and Other Fathers   202

Future Father   219

Foreword

Father Hunger

———

The women's movement has given birth to its most important child: the young but growing men's movement. When the first feminists started off on the long road to equality, they left behind not only the Marlboro Man, but a host of bewildered fathers, husbands, brothers, sons, and lovers. These men, finally forced to look at how the economic and social order devised by men had victimized, degraded, and stifled women, accepted the blame and began to try and right the wrongs of the past. Alan Alda replaced John Wayne as the new American hero, and the sensitive man was born.

This "journey into softness" and the development of men's feminine side has been valuable, says poet Robert Bly in *Iron John: A Book About Men,*[1] but more travel lies ahead. It is not enough to destroy the stereotypical macho man and replace him with the receptive male who recognizes and nurtures his feminine consciousness. "Both men and women are becoming disenchanted with the unisex ideal and are reclaiming the uniqueness of the sexes and exploring the differences between the genders," says social critic Sam Keen in *Fire in the Belly:*

On Being a Man.[2] The most common view of men and women in world mythology, he explains, "is that they are incarnations of separate but equal masculine and feminine cosmic principles—the yin and yang of things— that dovetail in all forms of creation."

In other words, men and women are different. Although this is immediately visible in their bodies, it is also visible under a microscope. Their brains are different. And because of this and the way we raise our boys and girls, their thought patterns and behaviors are different. But different does not mean unequal. We should acknowledge and take advantage of our differences rather than deny them in a futile attempt to make men and women the same in all ways.

Bly and Keen are at the forefront of a movement that is more than a backlash against feminism. Men are beginning to recognize the need for a new image of masculinity, and the '90s have been a constant reminder of men's inhumanity to women—the heavyweight boxing champion goes to jail for rape, a Supreme Court justice sits under a cloud of sexual harassment charges. Despite the obvious need for a new image of masculinity, men are having trouble creating that image because most of them were reared in the old tradition by men who could not teach them the values demanded in today's world. Even those who had the most attentive and loving fathers were reared in, and exposed to, society's sexist attitudes.

The men's movement is, in effect, a cry for the missing father, the father whose absence, indifference, workaholism, alcoholism, abuse, or stereotypical sexist attitudes permanently wounded his children by depriving them of a chance to be with an admirably masculine man and to learn from him. The missing ideal is not the savage macho man who dominated everyone and everything for thousands of years, but the heroic man of strength and virtue who protects and guides.

The men's movement traces this "father hunger" to the Industrial Revolution, which took the father out of the home and away from the family unit. As recently as 1900, most children grew up on farms with fathers and mothers providing separate masculine and feminine perspectives of humanity, but increasingly fathers became the missing element in the nuclear family. The mother became the power figure, and the image of the father was debased. He became either the weak and foolish Homer Simpson who has no control over his life or family or the brutal and cold stranger who returns from work too tired to offer guidance, support, or affection but not too tired to mete out the day's ration of punishment. Neither is an adequate father. Neither provides anything useful in terms of what it means to be a man. Daughters who grow up with such a father may never be able to fully trust a man. Sons who base their manhood on such an image will pass on the legacy of father hunger and poor parenting to their children.

Father hunger is not simply a figment of some poetic imagination or an excuse men can use to explain their fear of intimacy. It does exist, and it can be passed on from father to child. Proof of the existence of father hunger can be found in a growing number of studies that document the lack of connectedness between many fathers and sons. As part of one such study, for example, psychologist Samuel Osherson conducted in-depth interviews with men in their forties and found that most of them admitted to a lack of emotional closeness to both their fathers and their sons. In his book, *Finding Our Fathers: The Unfinished Business of Manhood*,[3] Osherson cites evidence suggesting that only 15 to 20 percent of American men experience a close, caring relationship with their fathers and argues convincingly that many of the problems men have in being intimate with their wives and children result from the lack of intimacy with their own fathers.

Despite mounting evidence for the importance of the father-child connection, many people still believe that Dad just provides a little extra and that kids get what they really need from Mom, starting with mother-child bonding at the breast. So how important are fathers anyway?

Some recent headlines from national papers offer some clues.

- Census Reveals Decline of the Traditional Family
- Quarter of Newborns in U.S. Were Born to Single Women
- Fragmented Families on Rise

These headlines announce the approaching death of the mother-father-child family. The articles under them go on to document the demise of the basic family unit with the latest census data. Ninety percent of single-parent families are headed by single women, and every decade more and more children are being reared without fathers. Even when their father is present, children may still be effectively fatherless because of his abuse, negligence, or inability to be close to them. And the situation is not confined to the inner cities or to the economically and socially deprived. It is spreading to the suburbs and is seen increasingly among rapidly divorcing younger couples.

Should we worry about the death of the family? Yes, research tells us that more and more children are growing up with only half of what they need and are likely to be only half of what they should be. For years, social scientists have been observing children and collecting vast amounts of information on what it means to grow up without fathers. They have been predicting everything from the vague feeling of sadness and malaise (a major factor in father hunger) to the outright social disaster of a generation of fatherless children who are sexually confused, socially inadequate, and intellectually and morally deprived.

Proof of these lacks is already known from studies of past generations. Spiraling divorce rates and an epidemic of out-of-wedlock pregnancies in the 1960s left millions of children to be reared by single mothers. When these children reached school age, teachers began to notice that they were not quite the same as children from homes with involved fathers. In general, the fatherless children tended to score lower than the others on intelligence, achievement, and aptitude tests.[4] Many of them also seemed to have social and personality problems; some were overly aggressive, whereas others were exceptionally shy and timid. These differences piqued the interest of child psychologists who soon found evidence that the early absence of a father is often associated with a wide range of problems, whereas close involvement with a father seems to increase the competence of young children.[5] Such findings encouraged researchers to take a systematic look at different kinds of father-child relationships and to investigate the impact men have on their children's lives. What they are finding makes it quite clear that fathers are just as important as mothers in all areas of children's lives. And given the relative lack of men in the lives of most children, from day care through grade school, a high level of involvement with a loving father can be especially important.[6]

One reason children without fathers lag in intellectual development is that they don't get as much attention and intellectual stimulation as children with two parents. But children need more than a second mother, more than extra stimulation. Despite Murphy Brown and the thousands of single women who have the time and money to give their children the best of everything, single mothers can't provide the unique kind of stimulation that fathers can offer. Beyond the obvious physical differences, men and women have distinct intellectual, social, and emotional styles. They tend to treat children differently and by doing so provide them with different ways of approaching life.

Just look at the way mothers and fathers behave when they drop their children off at day care. Researchers in Florida did just that and found that fathers are usually brisk and businesslike. They pat their kids on the back and send them off with a few words of encouragement about making new friends or learning new games. Mothers tend to hover and get emotional about leaving their toddlers with strangers. The first time a mother leaves her baby at day care, she is likely to hesitate, retrace her steps, or even return to give her baby just one more hug.[7] This well-intentioned behavior by a loving mother can actually trigger crying and fearfulness in the toddler. In this and in numerous other daily instances, fathers are often the encouragers, whereas mothers tend to be the comforters. And children need encouragement as much as they need comforting. An overprotected child probably will not experience as much freedom as other children to explore the world and develop the kind of self-assurance and independence that are the hallmarks of a healthy personality.

Obviously, many people who were deprived of their fathers grow up to be normal, healthy adults who lead normal, healthy lives and are more than adequate husbands and wives, mothers and fathers. They may have benefited from having the kind of mother who could cope with the challenges of single parenthood. They may have had older brothers, uncles, stepfathers, or male teachers who filled in the gaps in their lives. But considering all that can go wrong in families without fathers, there is little doubt that the father can and should be one of the most important factors in a child's life.

Many of the disastrous results predicted for children who grow up without fathers are based on studies of the most extreme cases of father absence, abuse, or neglect because, until recently, researchers have had little reason to study the positive influences fathers can have on their children. The mother has been and continues to be seen as the primary factor in a child's life. Most research on the family's role in child development has concentrated on the mother-child relationship, and many psychologists and therapists (and the parenting books they write) continue to ignore the father and emphasize the importance of the mother.[8] But now, a growing number of researchers and clinicians are looking more closely at the role of the father and concluding that leaving him out of child rearing is a serious mistake.

This mistake cannot be corrected, however, by simply having a man around the house. He has to be the kind of father who will not leave his children with a sense of father hunger, as many men in the past have done. The solution to father hunger is a new version of manhood, of fatherhood. This "new man" will be tender and emotional while still being strong and protective.[9] Consciousness raising and assertiveness training kept the women's movement rolling. Consciousness raising and sensitivity training may be necessary to get the men's movement in gear in order to help fathers fulfill this new ideal and, at the same time, pass it on through their children.

The immediate goal of the men's movement is to heal the wounds inflicted by the missing father, but the ultimate goal of the movement must be to ensure that the sins of the father are not visited on the next generation. It will be difficult for many men to overcome the past, but it is possible to shape the future. If we can't let go of all of our prejudices and ingrained ways of thinking, we can at least raise our children to meet the challenges set by the women's and men's movements. That is what *The Father Factor* can help us do. It is a parenting manual that recognizes the crucial role of the father in child and family development and provides guidelines for men and women who want to give their children the best of both the masculine and feminine worlds—the yin and the yang of it all. For the first time, one book pulls together all the available research on fathers and presents it in a way that helps fathers—*and mothers*—realize the importance of active, committed fathering. It explains how and why fathers and mothers are different and emphasizes the positive effects men can have on their children and families—from the time the decision to have a baby is made, through pregnancy, childbirth, infancy, childhood, and on into adolescence and adulthood. *The Father Factor* explains why the special qualities a man can bring to parenting are crucial in the intellectual, social, and sexual development of his sons and daughters and offers guidelines to help him overcome the obstacles society has placed on his road to fatherhood. It also suggests specific ways fathers can become more actively involved with their children and provides the information fathers need to answer the most important questions they have about fathering.

The Father Factor does not tell dads just to change diapers. Instead it emphasizes the importance of being there to change diapers. It explains the profound and lasting influences fathers have on their children and offers guidelines to help them be the best fathers they can be, the fathers many of them wish they had grown up with.

REFERENCES

1. Bly, R., *Iron John: A Book About Men*, Reading, MA: Addison-Wesley, 1990.

2. Keen, S., *Fire in the Belly: On Being a Man*. New York: Bantam Books, 1991.

3. Osherson, S., *Finding Our Fathers: The Unfinished Business of Manhood*. New York: Free Press, 1986.

4. Biller, H., and Salter, M., in D. Dietrich, and P. Shabad, (Eds.), *The Problem of Loss and Mourning: Psychoanalytic Perspectives*. New York: International Universities Press, 1989; Berlinsky, E., and Biller, H., *Parental Death and Psychological Development*. Lexington, MA: Lexington Books D.C. Heath, 1982.

5. Biller, H., and Solomon, R., *Child Maltreatment and Paternal Deprivation: A Manifesto for Research, Prevention and Treatment*. Lexington, MA: Lexington Books D.C. Heath, 1986.

6. Biller, H., *Fathers and Families: Paternal Factors in Child Development*, Westport, CT: Auburn House, 1993.

7. Gerwitz, J., and Pelaez-Nogueras, M., "Infant Protests: Protests During Maternal Departures and During Separations from Mothers as Conditioned Discriminative Operants," paper presented at the meeting of the American Psychological Association, San Francisco, 1991.

8. Biller, H. *Father, Child and Sex Role: Paternal Determinants of Personality Development*. Lexington, MA: Lexington Books D.C. Heath, 1971; *Paternal Deprivation: Family, School, Sexuality and Society*. Lexington, MA: Lexington Books D.C. Heath, 1974. Biller H., and Borstelmann, L., "Masculine Development: An Integrative Review." *Merrill-Palmer Quarterly*, Vol. 13, 1967, p. 253.

9. Biller, H., and Meredith, D. *Father Power*. New York: David McKay, 1974 (Doubleday Anchor Books, 1975).

SUGGESTED READINGS

FATHERHOOD AND FAMILIES IN CULTURAL CONTEXT by Bozett, F., and Hanson, S., (Eds.), Springer, 1991.

THE MALE EXPERIENCE by Doyle, J., Brown, 1991.

THE FATHER'S ROLE: CROSS-CULTURAL PERSPECTIVES by Lamb, M. (Ed.), Erlbaum, 1987.

FATHERHOOD IN AMERICA: A HISTORY by Griswold, R., Basic Books, 1993.

Introducing the Father Factor

WHAT'S A FATHER TO DO?

Having babies should be fun for fathers in the '90s. You get to go to childbirth classes and read piles of parenting books and magazines. If you want to, you get to meet your fetus via ultrasound and may even read stories and play music to the future apple of your eye. You buy the latest in educational geegaws to hang over the crib, stock up on Dr. Seuss books, and check out quality day-care options. When the blessed event arrives, you are there with your videocamera to record it for posterity.

If you are a father of the '90s, you and your wife are probably older and better educated than parents of the past. You plan to have fewer children and devote more time and energy to those you do have. Armed with reams of results from the recent boom in baby research, you are ready and willing to do everything possible to rear the perfect baby.

But then something happens. Mom and baby come home from the hospital, and perhaps your mother-in-law moves in to help out for a while. She and the new mom take charge. They know all there is to know about feeding and sleeping schedules, about changing diapers and burping babies. They hover and cuddle and coo, and you are left out in the cold. You may be the proud papa, but all you get to do is take pictures or take out the dirty diapers. When you do get to hold your bundle of joy or change a diaper, you get a stern warning: "Be careful. Not so rough. Keep the baby warm. Do it like I showed you."

Even if you aren't relegated to the sidelines of your baby's life and you and your wife agree that it is important for you to be closely involved with your child, society has conspired against you by placing almost the entire responsibility for parenting on women and by preparing girls, not boys, to be parents. Psychologist Ronald F. Levant, director of the Fatherhood Project in Boston, explains that "the current generation of fathers was socialized to be like their fathers. They did not play with dolls, nor mind their younger siblings, nor go to home economics classes, nor offer babysitting services to their neighbors. While our sisters visited nursing homes with their girl scout troops, we rubbed sticks together to make them burn".[1] In other words, says Levant, the current generation of men did not learn certain skills that most people associate with nurturing and caring for children, such as the ability to tune in to the feelings of others and how to become aware of, and express, their own feelings. Their sisters were taught to be sensitive to the feelings of others. They were taught to be aggressive and competitive. Genes and hormones certainly play a role in turning little boys into breadwinners and girls into homemakers (see Chapter 4), but society and many parents actively reinforce these roles. Despite this bias, fathers do have the potential to be as involved and nurturing as mothers. Their styles may be different, but the father's special participation contributes to the well-rounded development of their sons and daughters.

The women's movement helped women get out of the home and into the world of money and power and shifted part of parenting over to men, but little was actually done to help men be better fathers. Little really changed for men in terms of parenting roles. Society says fathers should be more involved with their children, but mothers still get custody of the children in 90 percent of divorce cases. Only 2 percent of the men eligible take advantage of paternity leave.[2] Many men say they want to spend more time with their children, but they don't. The average father spends less than thirty minutes per day with his infant. That plus a few hours on the weekend add up to about eight hours per week. Compare this with the enormous amount of time most mothers spend with their babies. Men in the '90s may be more aware of their responsibilities as fathers, but even relatively involved fathers spend less than one-third of the time mothers spend with their children, and only about one-fourth of that time is spent in one-on-one activities with children.[3] If a woman spent so little time with her children, she would be considered a negligent or inadequate mother. If she agreed to give up custody of her children, she would be called unnatural, morally defective, not a "mother" at all!

Despite this double standard, many fathers want to

be more actively involved as parents. And research shows clearly that they should. Child psychiatrist Kyle Pruett, for example, studied the children of men who stayed home while their wives went off to work and found that their sons and daughters not only thrive, they do much better than average.[4] When the infants were tested on problem-solving tasks during their first year of life, they performed at the level of infants six to twelve months older than they were. Their social skills were two to twelve months ahead of schedule. Why do these babies do so well? Pruett says it is the extra love and attention they get from having a closely involved father as well as a close and loving mother. The fathers and infants quickly formed deep attachments to each other, and the mothers—unlike many working fathers—also developed close attachments to their babies. These babies flourish, Pruett says, "because instead of having one and a quarter or one and a half parents, they have two real parents." When he tested the children two years later, they were still way ahead of the pack.

Unfortunately, most fathers can't or won't stay home to bring up baby, and even if they did, they simply wouldn't know how to do it. We keep hearing about the new man, the sensitive man of the '90s, but that man has yet to fully evolve. Sociologists and psychologists continue to report on the gender gap in intimacy. Most men still don't know how to get as closely involved with their children as they would like.[5] They may have a gut feeling about children needing more than mothering, more than hugging and feeding and dressing, but no one teaches them how to be intimate, empathetic, and involved with their children. No one teaches them how to give fully of themselves and provide the special qualities that men can bring to parenting, how to balance the mother's loving cautiousness with the kind of encouragement that leads to healthy assertiveness and self-confidence. The result is that most children get a lopsided view of the world. They get all the mothering they need—sometimes much more—but they don't get the full effect of the father's special brand of nurturance. They see how mothers react to and deal with the world, but they see little of how the other half does it. Most men don't even realize what it is they have to offer their children.

FATHERS AND SONS

One of the most important jobs of a father is to sow the seeds of wholesome masculinity in his son. In the '70s, feminists sensitized everyone to the destructive power of the traditionally limited, restrictive, and rigid sex-role stereotypes that handicapped both women and men. But even as certain aspects of our sex roles continue to evolve in response to the women's movement, it is clear that gender identity, the healthy acceptance of ourselves as males or females, remains a major part of our personalities. And an involved father has a direct impact on his son's positive acceptance of himself as masculine.

Identification and imitation are key concepts in understanding how young boys learn their concept of masculinity. The idea is that if your son loves you, he will identify with you and imitate your behavior. Freud said young boys first identify with their mothers, who provide food and comfort, and see their fathers as competitors for the mother's time and affection. More recent research puts fathers in a better light, suggesting that infants love their fathers and can be just as attached to them as to their mothers. Right from the beginning, babies are fascinated with your deeper voice, your stubby chin, the way you hold and play with them. They stare at you and get excited when you enter the room, and they may even prefer you to Mom when they aren't hungry. And if you are affectionate and rewarding, your son will want to be like you. It's only natural for a little boy to try to imitate someone who helps take care of him and makes him happy—someone who plays checkers with him after dinner, reads to him at bedtime, or takes him out for pizza after baseball or piano practice.

But you have to do more than provide a little fun for your son. It is especially important for your son to see you taking an active role in family affairs and in mother-father interactions. An involved father checks his children's homework. He doesn't simply ask if it is done. He doesn't work late or sit in front of the television while his wife handles all of the day-to-day decisions regarding the family. He asks about his children's activities and tells them about his. He invites them to do things with him as well as shares in their activities. He helps plan family meals, outings, and projects. He helps decide what time the kids should be home or who should clean the garage. He lets his children know that he is interested in every aspect of their lives, from school to work to play. And he is home enough of the time to take part in or oversee many of those activities. By being consistently involved, you show your son how to be appropriately assertive, independent, and competent. Adolescent boys who are insecure about themselves and their masculinity often come from homes in which the father played a passive role and did not participate in family decision making or in setting limits for his children. On the other hand, a father who is a tyrant, who is dominant, controlling, and restrictive, can damage his son's self-image and cause him to feel insecure about his own masculinity.[6] Fathers who are both masculine and nurturing, display an effective assertiveness, and are also closely involved with their sons foster a healthy sense of masculinity.

A loving father does more than foster positive masculinity in his son. Your care, attention, and encouragement are vital to your son's intellectual development. Studies of especially bright school-age boys, for example, have found that the underachievers tend to be those who had poor relationships with their fathers. Many of these men worked long hours and were rarely available to their sons. When they were home, they dominated and controlled their sons by means of excessive discipline and physical abuse. This kind of behavior can destroy a son's love and respect for his father and, in effect, take away a boy's desire to make his father proud of him.

Instead of trying to bully a boy into doing better, take an active interest in and encourage your son's intellectual pursuits. Seek him out and show your interest by asking questions and helping him in constructive ways. Don't do his homework for him but be available to offer suggestions, encouragement, and praise when he does his best. Involved fathers are especially likely to have sons who are strong in problem-solving abilities and have high grade-point averages.[7] Again, it is the quality of your behavior, particularly your loving acceptance of your son, that appears to be the important ingredient. When you spend time with your son, you expose him to what you know, what you have learned. You serve as a model and show him by your behavior that learning is important.

FATHERS AND DAUGHTERS

Many men say they would rather have a son than a daughter, not just because they want to pass on their names, but because they are afraid they won't know how to respond to a girl. Often, their fear is justified. But girls need fathers just as much as boys do—and for many of the same reasons. Boys model their masculinity on their fathers, and girls learn how to feel positive about their femininity from their fathers. By watching and interacting with their fathers, girls learn how to react to males and how males will react to their femininity.

Researchers long ago observed that in many families it is the father, not the mother, who is the principal transmitter of our ideas of masculinity and femininity. Men, for example, are more likely than women to emphasize sex differences in the way they treat their children. And this begins in the first days of life. Mothers tend to treat infant boys and girls the same. They love and nurture them. Fathers are more likely to treat boys and girls differently. They roughhouse and play more aggressively, in general, with their sons and encourage more assertive behavior. Unfortunately, many fathers have overly rigid sex-role stereotypes and, in their zeal to feminize their daughters, actively discourage the development of assertiveness and intellectual competence.

The best way to foster competence in your daughter and give her a positive feeling about being a female is to encourage and appreciate both her social and intellectual achievements. Encourage her so-called feminine traits— her expressiveness, warmth, and sensitivity—but also encourage and reward her assertiveness, independence, and achievements. Women who have both positive feminine and positive masculine characteristics are the women most likely to reach their fullest potential. Women who have pride in their femininity and are independent and assertive as well as nurturing and sensitive are likely to be socially and intellectually successful, whether they become homemakers or choose a career.[8]

Your close involvement with your daughter is especially important because it is you, not your wife, who has the greatest influence on her ability to relate to men. By being closely involved, you give her the chance to compare her femininity with your masculinity and to have her femininity rewarded by a man who is special in her life. And the way you react to your daughter's sexuality and femininity can have lasting effects on the way she relates to men. A girl who is constantly frustrated in her interactions with her father may develop a negative attitude toward men. Women who have difficulty maintaining intimate relationships with men tend to come from homes in which there was a poor father-daughter relationship. Women who are successful in their career pursuits as well as successful wives and mothers are more likely to come from homes in which both parents were positively involved. But the quality of the father-daughter relationship is crucial if a woman is to be successful in both her relationships with men and her creative and professional life. Most such women had fathers who were personally secure, vital, and achievement oriented. They treated their daughters with respect and valued their basic femininity, but they also expected their daughters to develop their abilities whether or not they coincided with accepted sex-role stereotypes.

FATHERS AND MOTHERS

Any explanation of how you influence your children must include your relationship with their mother. Constant conflict and poor husband-wife communication, for instance, distort a child's view of male-female relationships. Children in such families may not learn to deal well with members of the other sex. On the other hand, if you and your wife satisfy and value each other, if you communicate with and respect each other, your children will have the opportunity to learn how to deal effectively with others.

In the best of all worlds, children will have both an involved mother and an involved father. But an involved father does more than foster healthy social development in his children. Your commitment to shared parenting is a key factor in both your wife's happiness and in her ability to be a good mother. Even before the birth of a child, your emotional support contributes to your wife's health and sense of well-being. Women who have supportive husbands are more likely to have a relatively problem-free pregnancy and delivery and to be more competent in nursing and caring for their infants and young children. And once the child is born, your close involvement in child care can be a factor in your wife's mental health. Researchers Catherine E. Ross and John Mirowsky interviewed more than 600 couples to find out who took care of the children and how often each parent had experienced various symptoms of depression. When child care was the woman's responsibility and help hard to obtain, the women were depressed twice as often as the men. But the researchers found that if fathers share part of the child-care duties, the mother is depressed much less often. And taking part in child care doesn't seem to cause the men any undue stress. When fathers shared child-care responsibilities, their levels of depression did not go up.[9]

Your close involvement in family life also contributes to your wife's personal development and effectiveness outside the home. Too many mothers in two-parent as well as one-parent families suffer greatly because of the lack of involvement of fathers. Employed mothers often find themselves doing the equivalent of two full-time jobs because their husbands take relatively little responsibility for child rearing. But if you are actively involved in your family, you can liberate your wife from many of her worries. If you show her that you are a caring, responsible father, she will trust you to watch the children and feel free to pursue goals outside the home. And if you truly value her outside activities, she will be much happier in her career and with her family life. Many employed mothers actually spend more quality, one-on-one time with their children than do those who stay at home. In other words, your close involvement can help your wife become a better parent and a better person.

Moreover, getting involved with your kids, whether playing catch or lending a sympathetic ear, is as good for you as it is for your children and wife. The more you invest in your family, the better off you and they will be in later life. The benefits of fatherhood can be seen in a study that looked at the effect of fatherhood on the careers and psychological growth of 200 fathers over four decades.[10] You may think your career will suffer if you put a lot of extra time and effort into your family, but the researchers found that fatherhood did not harm the men's work lives. "They may have delayed writing a paper or put off some other project, but in the long run involved fathers went just as far in their work as comparable men did who were less involved with their kids." In related studies, the researchers also found evidence suggesting that fathers who have close relationships with their children report fewer physical ailments and symptoms of psychological distress than do men who do not have satisfying relationships with their children.[11]

Finally, the researchers found that the more fathers nurtured their children socially and emotionally, the more giving and caring these men were when they reached middle age. Fathers who actively promoted their own children's development, taking them trick-or-treating or advising them on dating problems, were likely to assume responsibilities outside their families in later life. These men had achieved what psychoanalyst Erik Erikson calls the stage of generativity, the peak of maturity. Their involvement with their children carried over to later life where they continued to contribute to the growth of the next generation, whether it be by coaching a team or by serving on a school board.

Along with your children and their mother, you can also experience the full benefits of being a committed, competent, and loving father. In the following chapters you will start on a unique and fulfilling journey to effective parenting. Drawing on recent and relevant research, we provide the information and insights men and women need to answer their questions about the role of the father in family life. In this parenting manual, unlike so many others, we emphasize the crucial role fathers *should* play in child and family development and offer guidelines for men and women who want to share parenting responsibilities while boosting competence in themselves and their children. *The Father Factor* does for men what all other parenting books have done for women. It puts fathers back in the nuclear family.

- Chapter 2 helps you examine your reasons for wanting to become a father and suggests ways you can prepare to be the best father possible.
- Chapter 3 looks at pregnancy and the importance to your wife that you play your role as a full partner in pregnancy.
- Chapter 4 focuses on your ability to form a close bond with your newborn child and your crucial role in your infant's development.
- Chapter 5 is about toddlers and the stages through which you can expect to see your child progress.

- Chapters 6 and 7 explain your role in the intellectual and moral development of your children as they progress through childhood. The focus is on your role in helping your children develop positive body image, self-esteem, moral standards, and intellectual and social competence.
- Chapter 8 is about teenagers and a father's special contribution to social and sexual development.
- Chapter 9 looks at divorce, single fathers, and stepfathers and the advantage of a man's continued involvement with his children even if he does not live with them.
- Chapter 10 looks to the future and your role as a grandfather and a social father—a man who feels his responsibility to all the children of the world.

REFERENCES

1. Levant, R., "Emotional Self-Awareness in Men," paper presented at the meeting of the American Psychological Association, San Francisco, 1991.

2. U.S. Bureau of Labor Statistics, cited in the *Washington Post*, July 7, 1992.

3. Biller, H., and Solomon, R., *Child Maltreatment and Paternal Deprivation: A Manifesto for Research, Prevention and Treatment*. Lexington, MA: Lexington Books/D.C. Heath, 1986.

4. Pruett, K., Stay-Home Fathers' Superkids, *Psychology Today*, January 1983, p. 71.

5. Osborne, R., Men and Intimacy: An Empirical Review, paper presented at the meeting of the American Psychological Association, San Francisco, 1991.

6. Biller, H., The Father and Sex Role Development, in M. Lamb (Ed.), *The Role of the Father is Child Development*. New York: Wiley, 1981.

7. Biller, H., and Salter, M., in D. Dietrich and P. Shabad

(Eds.), *The Problem of Loss and Mourning: Psychoanalytic Perspectives*. New York: International Universities Press, 1989.

8. Biller, H., *Fathers and Families: Paternal Factors in Child Development*. Westport, CT: Auburn House, 1993.

9. Ross, C., and Mirowsky, J., Why Parents Should Share Child Care, *Psychology Today*, March 1989, p. 58.

10. Roberts, M., The Benefits of Fatherhood, *Psychology Today*, March 1989, p. 76.

11. Barnett, C., Marshall, N., and Pleck, J., Men's Multiple Roles and Their Relationship to Men's Psychological Distress, in *Journal of Marriage and the Family* vol. 54, 1992, p. 858.

SUGGESTED READINGS

FATHERS AND FAMILIES; PATERNAL FACTORS IN CHILD DEVELOPMENT by Biller, H., Auburn House, 1993.

WRESTLING WITH LOVE; HOW MEN STRUGGLE WITH INTIMACY, WITH WOMEN, CHILDREN, PARENTS, AND EACH OTHER by Osherson, S., Fawcett, 1992.

THE MOTHER PUZZLE: A NEW GENERATION RECKONS WITH MOTHERHOOD by Schwartz, J., Simon & Schuster, 1993.

HOW FATHERS CARE FOR THE NEXT GENERATION: A FOUR DECADES STUDY by Snarey, J., Harvard University Press, 1993.

So You Want to Be a Daddy

Bam! Ed punched out the storm door window when he got the news. Twenty years later he's still got scars on his knuckles to remind him of how he had screwed up his life. Lisa, the high school girl he had dated for several months, came crying to his door to tell him she was pregnant, and Ed saw his life going down the tubes. He was eighteen years old, had just started college, had several new girlfriends, and was looking forward to four years of fun and then medical school. The last thing he wanted was to be tied down with a wife and a kid. He didn't know anything about babies. He didn't want to quit school. He didn't want to start working full-time at the supermarket. But he was trapped. So he did what his parents and her parents told him was the right thing. It soon became apparent that Ed wasn't ready for marriage or fatherhood.

Looking back he says, "Do you know what it is like to live with a pregnant woman you barely know and aren't even sure you love? I worked ten hours a day and couldn't even go out for a beer after work. I had to go straight home and clean up after a bulging wife who acted like she was helpless. Sometimes, she wouldn't even get out of bed for two or three days. Then there were the times she went crazy. I'd try to give her some rational excuse for why I was late, and she wouldn't even listen. She'd run around the house, screaming and yelling, and I didn't even know why. I thought she wanted to kill me—or herself and the baby. I don't know if it was hormones or what that made her act like a madwoman. All I know is that I could barely stand to be in the same room with her. I started coming home later and later every night.

"Lisa wasn't even sure she wanted to be pregnant at first. She said she didn't want to lose her figure or be saddled with a baby, but once she began to feel the baby kick, her attitude really changed. She got into the mommy mode, began shopping for baby clothes, and looking for a larger apartment. We argued constantly. She wanted me to do all the shopping and housework. I wanted to go out with the guys—and gals. Lisa nagged me to work even longer hours so we could afford a larger apartment. I hated my job. And no sex! We used to make love all the time, anywhere we could when we first met, but not when she was pregnant. She always came up with some lame excuse—nausea, a backache, or she was tired or uncomfortable.

"And things only got worse after the baby came. Lisa

was depressed for months, and the baby cried all the time. I loved my little girl, but Lisa acted like she was the mother of all mothers. She barely let me touch the baby and made me feel awkward and clumsy every time I tried to change her or just play with her. She wouldn't even leave me alone with my baby girl.

"Lisa eventually got into a better mood, and things calmed down for a while. But then it happened again. Another baby was on the way, and the same problems arose—with a vengeance. By the time our third baby was born, I had had it. I felt my life was out of control, and I knew I was making things worse by taking out my frustrations on Lisa and the kids. I started seeing other women, my marriage was a failure, family life was intolerable for everyone, and after ten long years I moved out."

Ed is like many of us. He's in his late thirties now, and he is planning to raise a second family. He tried to do the right thing the first time around, but he just wasn't ready. His story is familiar. The divorce rate for parents younger than eighteen is three times higher than for couples who have their first child after they are twenty.[1] And more than twice as many divorced as married people knew their partner for less than a year before they got married.[2]

But teenage boys aren't the only ones who take on the job of fatherhood before they are ready. Most men have little or no idea of what they are getting into. They know almost nothing about pregnancy, childbirth, babies, or the awesome responsibilities they are about to assume.

Ed knows. Now. He eventually finished college, got a decent job, and sees his kids on a regular basis. He's grown up a lot, married again, and has decided to start a second family at the age of thirty-nine. "This time," he says, "I know what I'm getting into, and I know I'll do it right." And he probably will. He and his new wife thought long and hard about having children, and they are ready and willing to share equally in the joys and inevitable frustrations that come with parenthood.

TO BE OR NOT TO BE?

Fatherhood comes as a surprise to many men, but considering its importance, it is a responsibility you should take on only when you are sure you are ready for what will probably be more than a twenty-year emotional and financial commitment, and when your reasons for wanting to be a father are valid. If you are like most men, you probably want to have children because they are a link with the future, a chance to influence society and to have part of your personality live on after you. Nobody wants to be a genetic dead end. You probably also dream of having a close, loving relationship with a child you will love and be proud of, a child who loves and respects you. And this will probably be the case. Most young adults see their parents as heroes and heroines. When psychologist Frank Farley asked 340 college students to rank their top five heroes and heroines, the usual names came up: Jesus, John F. Kennedy, Martin Luther King, Mother Theresa, Amelia Earhart, Madonna, but the overwhelming winners were parents. Moms got six times as many first-place votes as did any other heroine, and dads got twice as many as any other hero.[3] But don't expect to be a hero all the time. If you look back at your own childhood, you will begin to realize that the rewards of fatherhood come with a great many difficulties and responsibilities, stresses and frustrations.

- Ask yourself why you want to be a father. Be sure that you really do and that your reasons are valid. If you don't feel ready for fatherhood, don't do it just because your wife wants to have children or because your parents want to be grandparents.
- Don't become a father because you want to prove you can do it better than your parents did. The everything-I-didn't-have syndrome can backfire. You can't and probably shouldn't give your child everything you didn't have.
- Like everyone else, you have some limit on how many people you can share yourself with fully. Think about this as you decide to have a child, especially if it is your second, third, or even sixth child.
- Remember that your genetic contribution is just as important as your wife's. Make sure you are physically ready to be a father before you even try to conceive a child. Avoid alcohol, drugs, and cigarettes even before trying to conceive a child. Studies indicate that alcohol and drugs can interfere with your ability to produce a healthy child. Newborn infants of men who drink excessively, for example, weigh less than those of non-drinkers.[4] There is also evidence that cocaine molecules become attached to sperm and may then harm the embryo. Women who use cocaine often during pregnancy have infants with severe problems because the fetus is exposed to the drug throughout pregnancy, but it is possible that cocaine on your sperm could lead to subtle deficits, such as learning disabilities and memory problems.

The next question you should ask before deciding to become a father has to do with the quality of your relationship with your wife. One of the most important

things you can do for your children is to love their
mother. If you and your wife have a loving and sharing
relationship, you are probably ready to share in the joys
and responsibilities of parenthood. If your relationship
is weak or if you and your wife have difficulties communicating with each other, it is probably best to postpone
parenthood until your marriage is more stable. Taking
the time to work out your differences increases the
chances both of you will be ready for the challenge of
parenthood.

Whatever you do, don't have a baby only because
you think it will strengthen your relationship. The
stresses of parenthood can further weaken a troubled
relationship. Even if you and your wife have a secure
partnership, parenthood can take a toll on your marriage, as psychologist Jay Belsky and his colleagues
found. Since 1980, they have interviewed and observed
more than 250 families, beginning three months before
the birth of a child and at various times over the year
following birth. They ask how happy the marriage is,
how the couples divide up household and child-care
chores, and whether the couples feel their marriage is a
romance, a friendship, or a partnership. The results are
pretty much what you would expect. The quality of a
marriage usually declines with the birth of a child. During the first year most couples report increasing dissatis-
faction with their relationship. For many, it becomes
more of a job and less of a romance. And the mothers
get the worst of it. Despite the men's apparent willing-
ness to share, most of the women still find themselves
doing much more than half of the housework and child
care.[5]

- Discuss your relationship with your wife. Air both
  positive and negative feelings, and bring up any con-

cerns either of you might have about the future of your relationship and address them early in your marriage.

- Discuss how you both feel about having children and how you would like to rear them. Your decision should be made jointly and should be based on both of your attitudes toward child rearing.
- Consider your own and your wife's educational and career goals as well as your financial situation before deciding to start or add to your family.
- If you do not feel that you are ready to have children, put off starting a family. The extra time will be good for you, your wife, and your future children. Your wife may feel that she has to beat the biological time clock, but unless she is nearing menopause, she probably has time to spare. More and more women are postponing parenting until they are in their mid thirties, and according to maternal-fetal medicine specialist Kenneth Moiset, they have healthier pregnancies and babies than do younger mothers.[6] Consider putting off pregnancy until both of your careers are on solid foundations. Typically, women who postpone pregnancy until their thirties are better educated than those who get pregnant in their late teens or early twenties. They take better care of themselves, exercise regularly, and have healthier diets. They also tend to go for prenatal care earlier and more often and are more likely to follow the doctor's instructions and recommendations.
- If you already have one or more young children, be especially aware of how successful you and your wife have already been as parents.
- Don't feel that you have to be completely enthusiastic about having a child. Many expectant fathers, especially first-timers, are anxious about their ability to love and support an infant. Many feel that they will be trapped, that they will have to give up all their free

time. Discuss these fears with your wife. Trying to deny them can lead to even more anxiety.

- If you and your wife have a troubled marriage and don't communicate well with each other, seek professional help from someone with training in family counseling and parenting issues.

Another good way to predict how ready you are to be a good father is to look back at your own childhood, at your parents and how they treated you. Did you have a close, supportive relationship with both your parents? If so, you have good examples to follow and should have the kind of attitude it takes to be a good father. Did you have parents who were fun to be with but who failed to give you the emotional support and guidance you felt you needed? Perhaps you can learn from what you see as their mistakes.

As an adult you may be more accepting of your relationship with your parents, but you may still have a great deal of ambivalence toward them. For many people, there is no choice but to confront painful childhood issues if they are ever to be loving and effective parents. The thought of becoming a father should encourage you to deal with any problems you had with your parents and enable you to realistically evaluate them, with all their strengths and weaknesses, for the first time. As Samuel Osherson suggests in *Finding Our Fathers*, if you don't come to terms with past relationships, especially with your parents, you may be condemned to reproduce them.[7] We become, in effect, the parents we swore we would never be. Here are some things you can do to stimulate your thinking and confront these issues:

- Get out your old family photo album and try to remember as much as you can about your parents and your childhood—the good times and the bad. Think about the kind of parenting you received and the kind of parent you want to be. What influenced you most about each of your parents and about their relationship with one another? Consider their personalities and values, and compare yourself with them.

- Talk to your parents about how they felt about you, about how they felt about their own parents. Remind them of all the good times and the bad times, and encourage them to recall times they felt especially close to or distant from you. A heart-to-heart talk with each of your parents can provide insights that were not apparent to any of you ten or twenty years earlier. Analyzing past conflicts with your parents and looking at them from both sides will improve your ability to empathize with your own children.

- Watch how your father treats his grandchildren. If he is older than fifty, his hormone levels are probably going down and he is likely to be much more mellow than he was when you were a child. He is likely to have the time and patience to take a real interest in his grandchildren and deal with them compassionately. If so, it is not too late to learn from your father. (For more on grandfathers, see Chapter 10.)

OFF TO DADDY SCHOOL

Ed's prediction that he would get it right the second time is coming true. Not only is he better off emotionally, educationally, and financially, but he has also been married for several years to a woman he knows he wants to have children with. He knows what pregnancy, childbirth, and babies are all about, and he is sure he will be able to cope this time.

Ed learned from his mistakes, but fatherhood is something you want to get right the first time. Fatherhood is so important that everyone should probably have to take special courses, pass a test, and get a license before they are put in charge of an infant. Cab drivers, scuba divers, even soil testers, have to get licensed. Why not parents? Now, almost anyone can take a stab at it. Only adoption agencies investigate the qualifications of prospective parents.

Of course, the brave new world of fatherhood doesn't require a license, but the idea of fatherhood training is one whose time has definitely come, especially since young boys and men in our society don't usually have much contact with infants. Until they have their own children, or at least until they become expectant fathers, men usually don't even show much interest in infants. The next time somebody brings a baby into a group, watch how the men and women react. The women will probably crowd around and admire the baby and want to hold it. The men may smile and say how cute the baby is but will usually keep their distance and won't appear overly enthusiastic. This doesn't mean that men can't be interested in babies. It means that most of us learned, by the time we were four or five years old, that babies and dolls are what girls play with. Many young boys even have to repress any natural interest in babies in order to appear masculine.[8]

This situation, however, may be changing. Education for Parenting, for example, is a Philadelphia-based organization that teaches parenting classes in elementary schools. Carefully chosen volunteer parents bring their infants or toddlers into fifth- and sixth-grade classrooms once a month so that the students can watch and record the behavior of the parents and babies and then describe the results. Students weigh and measure the babies and chart their development. They learn how to solve parent-child problems in positive ways and how to help babies grow intellectually. They get to play with the babies and learn to explore and express their own nurturing and empathetic responses to them. Students who have taken the course have been tested and, compared with untrained students, found to be much more knowledgeable about early child development. They also were able to think up more nurturant and positive solutions to common parent-child problems and were less likely to suggest physical punishment. Researchers expect this kind of training to carry over into later years, making these students better parents.[9]

You probably never had a course like that when you were in school. But even if the announcement that you are about to be a father comes as a surprise, you still have several months to learn your new job. Parenting and fathering courses are becoming increasingly available, and researchers are finding that even simple, short-term courses can have long-term effects on the way fathers approach child rearing. In one such program, designed by psychologist Ross Parke and his coworkers, new fathers visiting their wives in the hospital were asked to watch a videotape that focuses on father–infant interactions, child care, and the social and learning abilities of infants. The tape emphasizes the importance of fathers being active participants in the care and stimulation of even very young infants. Men who watched the tape compared with those who had not seen it were more willing to take care of their babies and to play with them. Three months later, these men were more likely than the others to be regularly involved in feeding and changing diapers and, in general, seemed to be more in tune with the needs of their babies.[10]

In another experiment, psychologist Milton Kotelchuck and his co-workers taught relatively noninvolved fathers how to play appropriately with their infants. These men got to watch another man play skillfully with an infant and received coaching as they played with their own babies for thirty minutes a day over a four-week period. These men became more active with their infants compared with untrained fathers, and their infants began to take more interest in them.[11] When this happened, some mothers began to encourage more father involvement while decreasing their own level of involvement, giving the babies a better balance between Mom and Dad.

- One of the first things you should do after deciding to become a father is to find out what kind of parenting or fathering courses are available to you and then enroll in one with your wife. If you can't find one, contact the Fatherhood Project, which acts as a clearinghouse for information on fathering programs and services across the country and is helping increase awareness of the importance of men and women sharing equally in parenting responsibilities. Call (212) 268-4846.
- The next thing you should do is get to know some babies. Go on family outings with friends or relatives who have young children. Offer to baby-sit. Perhaps you and your wife can even borrow a baby for a weekend to get an idea of what you are in for. But don't expect to be infatuated by children just by having more contact with them. And remember that simply playing with children or baby-sitting is not all there is to being a parent. Nevertheless, spending some time being responsible for an infant, especially if you are inexperienced, is a good way to start your preparation for fatherhood.

▪ Take a close look at the fathers and mothers among your family and friends. What kind of parents are they? What do they do that you admire? Where have they had difficulties and, in your opinion, made mistakes? But don't make rash judgments. You may vow never to become overwhelmed by your job and neglect your children but may later find yourself coming home every night with a bulging briefcase.

AND BABY MAKES THREE, FOUR, FIVE . . .

It used to be part of the American Dream: a bread-winning dad presiding at the head of the table, a bread-baking mom at the other end, and a brood of happy kids in between. It makes for a great Norman Rockwell painting, but having a large family does not make your job as a parent any easier, especially if you are serious about developing high-quality personal relationships with each of your children. Every additional child increases demands on your time and takes a little away from the quality of parenting for each child. Additional children also dilute the learning environment and thus affect each child's intellectual development.[12] And when children are close in age, it becomes even more difficult for parents to treat them as individuals and maintain a special relationship with each of them.

Close spacing also increases the likelihood of problems among children and makes it difficult for them to develop positive relationships with each other. Almost all children under the age of four, especially those who already have a difficult temperament, are likely to be upset when they have to begin sharing their parents with a new brother or sister. They become more disobedient and demanding and, in general, act more like infants themselves. Researchers have found, however, that children who have a close relationship with their fathers are much less likely to have severe and long-lasting problems in response to the birth of a new baby than are those who are close only to their mothers. When there is only one loving parent, the older child has no one to turn to when the mother begins to devote most of her time to the infant.[13]

You can't completely prevent feelings of anger and jealousy between your children, but you can contribute to a better family atmosphere by responding to each child's needs for attention and by praising them when they do get along instead of focusing on their rivalry. Children usually continue to have some mixed feelings about their younger brothers or sisters, but in most families, there is also much playful and positive interaction among children. Most firstborns will also show some interest in helping take care of younger children and feel affection and empathy for them. In one study, researchers watched what happened when young children, most around four years old, were left alone with their infant brothers or sisters. Most of the infants cried when the parent left the room, but within ten seconds more than half of the older children made an attempt to comfort the babies by reassuring them, picking them up, or distracting them with toys. Older brothers were likely to give only as much care as the baby seemed to need, whereas older sisters tended to give far more attention than the baby seemed to need. The researchers suggest that this may have to do with parental behavior, with boys imitating the less involved care-giving styles of their fathers and girls imitating the overindulgence of their mothers.[14]

- Discuss the advantages and disadvantages of having a large family before making the decision to have an additional child. Make sure you and your wife can really be committed to each child before you decide to enlarge your family. If possible, try to space your children four or more years apart so that you get to know each child without being overwhelmed by diapers and sibling rivalry.

- If you are an involved father, your time commitments must increase with the number of children you have. But you don't have to spend twice as much time with two children, three times as much with three, and so on. Divide your day so that each child has some special time with you in addition to being with you in more general family activities. For instance, if you have three young children, spend some time each day talking and playing with them as a group, but make sure you save some time to spend alone with each child. Try to make sure that every child gets a special outing away from the rest of the family at least once a week. As a rule, younger children are much more in need of daily special times than are children of nine or ten who feel quite satisfied with some of your attention every other day or so.[15]

- Encourage your older children to help out with the younger ones, but do not force them to become junior parents. Be appreciative of the help you receive, but don't pressure them to give up activities that they enjoy just to take care of a new baby. The best way to encourage older children to love and care for their younger brothers and sisters is by your own example of kindness and caring, not by demanding or ordering them to take care of the baby.

- Beware of birth-order bias. Researchers polled 275

people and found that most adults have some very prejudiced ideas about children. Firstborns are seen by many people as achievers, and because more is expected of them, they are often criticized for not living up to unrealistic expectations. Only children are often seen as school-minded, self-centered, and spoiled. Lastborns are seen as sociable, disobedient, and nonacademic. Because half the people in the study were parents and half were not, the researchers suggest that these beliefs are not based on actual experiences with children but on stereotypes passed on from generation to generation. Regardless of whether such biased beliefs have a basis in fact, they can become self-fulfilling prophesies.[16]

Ed's doing fine now, and so are both of his families. He still has his scars, but he's a changed man—and his children did it. Ed has matured and softened. His hormones aren't raging like they were when he was first married, and he doesn't feel that he has to conquer every new woman he meets. He's no longer bitter about having had to miss out on medical school. He's happy with his job and less ambitious than he once was. He's willing to devote more attention to his family this time around. Not living with his children after the divorce made him realize what an important part of his life they had become. Seeing them only on alternate weekends forced him to pay more attention to their special qualities and needs and to try to make up for lost time. He's willing to do that full time for his new family right from the start.

REFERENCES

1. Robinson, B., and Barret, R., Teenage Fathers, *Psychology Today*, December 1985, p. 70.

2. Kohn, A., You Know What They Say. . . , *Psychology Today*, April 1988, p. 40.

3. Stark, E., Mom and Dad: The Great American Heroes, *Psychology Today*, May 1986, p. 12.

4. Skerrett, P., Blame It on Your Father, *OMNI*, September 1991, p. 36.

5. Roberts, M., A Parent Is Born, *Psychology Today*, December 1986, p. 18.

6. *Washington Post* June 30, 1992, Health Section, p. 5.

7. Osherson, S., *Finding Our Fathers: The Unfinished Business of Manhood*. New York: Free Press, 1986.

8. Miedzian, M., *Boys Will Be Boys, Breaking the Link Between Masculinity and Violence*. New York: Doubleday, 1991.

9. Masterpasqua, F., "Teaching Children About Parenting," paper presented at the meeting of the American Psychological Association, Washington, DC, August 1992.

10. Parke, R., and Beitel, A., in M. Lamb (Ed.), *The Father's Role, Applied Perspectives*. New York: Wiley, 1986.

11. Kotelchuck, M., in M. Lamb (Ed.), *The Role of the Father in Child Development*. New York: Wiley, 1976.

12. Zuckerman, D., Too Many Sibs Put Our Nation at Risk? *Psychology Today*, January 1985, p. 5.

13. Biller, H., *Fathers and Families: Paternal Factors in Child Development*. Westport, CT: Auburn House, 1993.

14. Guinzburg, S., Siblings' Motherly Concern, *Psychology Today*, March 1984, p. 8.

15. Biller, H. and Meredith, D., *Father Power*. New York: David McKay, 1974; Doubleday Anchor Books, 1975.

16. Stark, E., Birth-Order Bias, *Psychology Today*, August 1985, p. 13.

SUGGESTED READINGS

THE SIX STAGES OF PARENTHOOD by Galinsky, E., Addison-Wesley, 1987.

THE BIRTH OF A FATHER by Greenberg, M., Avon, 1985.

THINGS JUST HAVEN'T BEEN THE SAME: MAKING THE TRANSITION FROM MARRIAGE TO PARENTHOOD by Sachs, B., Morrow, 1992.

3

The Pregnant Father

To the proud parents, especially the mother who did all the work!

Jerrold Lee Shapiro, a family therapist, got the above card after the birth of his daughter, and he says its sentiment sums up an entire cultural phenomenon. "We truly value motherhood and child rearing. We pamper pregnant women. . . . Our culture loses its paranoia and its boundaries in the presence of pregnancy." And this is as it should be. A woman is more vulnerable when she is pregnant and clearly deserves special attention and support. But what about her husband? Emotionally and psychologically, Shapiro says, he is as pregnant as she is, yet there is a contradiction. Our society expects fathers to play an increasingly larger role in pregnancy and birth but tells them to keep their emotions and their fears to themselves.

Shapiro's experiences as a new father prompted him to take a closer look at the pregnant father. He interviewed and tested 227 expectant and recent fathers and found that many of them were just as anxious and concerned about pregnancy as their wives were. Medical matters, for example, are a major source of discomfort to many men, most of whom know little or nothing about obstetrics and gynecology. Several men who went with their wives to prenatal pelvic exams told Shapiro that they were ignored and treated as if they were in the way by the same doctors who had previously praised them for being so involved.

Most men reported fears of losing their wives during childbirth and worries that their child would be born damaged in some way. Such fears are quite natural. Only fifty years ago, childbirth complications were a major cause of death among young women. Times and medical care have changed, but the fear lingers.

Eighty percent of the men also reported concerns about the increased financial responsibility that comes with an extra mouth to feed. Shapiro says he found himself unconsciously letting his private practice expand while his wife was pregnant. Other men told him of switching to more reliable jobs or taking on a second job to earn more money. Many men also feared that they would be replaced by the new baby and left out of the relationship. The most common fear that expectant fathers had was that they would not be able to handle the birth process, would get sick at the sight of blood, or would not be able to really help their wives through the delivery. Despite these fears, most men find the birth experience fascinating and wonderful and get through it with no problem.

The apprehension and anxiety that many pregnant men feel is quite natural, says Shapiro, and they need to share their fears with their wives. Most of the fathers he talked to, however, had kept their fears to themselves rather than further burdening their pregnant wives. Unfortunately, he says, this just isolates them and makes close emotional connections more difficult to achieve. The men who did share their worries with their wives found that their marriages grew deeper and closer.

> If fathers are to get a solid psychological start on parenthood, Shapiro concludes, they must learn to accept their natural fears during pregnancy. If men are to be involved in prenatal matters, their own negative feelings must be accepted by others. A cultural double bind that only partially and grudgingly accepts men's participation in pregnancy and birth restricts intimacy between partners at a time when both of them need more communication rather than less. . . . The father-to-be cannot be fully a part of the pregnancy and birth unless these fears are fully recognized by himself, by his spouse, by his family and by society in general.[1]

Some men get so anxious and emotionally involved in their wife's pregnancy that they actually begin to act and feel like they are pregnant. Approximately 15 to 20 percent of fathers-to-be develop symptoms similar to those of their pregnant wives. They may have abdominal pains, loss of appetite, indigestion, nausea, vomiting, weight gain, backaches, insomnia, and a sense of constant agitation. A few even become bedridden toward the end of their wife's pregnancy. Such symptoms are usually laughed at by family and friends, but men who get sick or have sympathetic labor pains may have had little contact with their own fathers and come to identify closely with their pregnant wives in order to begin to feel like a parent. Shapiro suggests that these men may be unconsciously compensating for the fact that our culture still leaves men pretty much out of the pregnancy picture. When was the last time you were invited to a baby shower for an expectant father? The jokes about men who have physical reactions to their wife's pregnancy, Shapiro says, are just another indication of society's indifference to the feelings of the expectant father.

It hasn't always been that way. In many ancient societies, it was customary for new fathers to take to their beds at the time of birth and simulate the symptoms of labor and childbirth. They would moan and thrash about, receive gifts from family and friends, go on a strict diet, and be told to rest. This curious custom is known as *couvade* (from the French word meaning "to hatch"). Its social function seems to be to emphasize the role of the father in reproduction. It is also possible that imitating the mother's labor and birth pains increases the father's empathy and compassion. And by becoming a partner in his wife's pregnancy and pain, he actually reduces her physical pain.

PARTNERS IN PREGNANCY

When you and your wife got married, you became partners in life. When you and your wife conceived a child, you became partners in pregnancy. To be an effective partner you must be as closely involved as possible in every stage of the pregnancy—from the choice of an obstetrician to the moment of birth. Obviously, you won't be as physically involved as your wife. Your belly won't swell, your hormones won't fluctuate, and you probably won't get morning sickness or have labor pains.

But you can stay emotionally close to your wife and try to experience with her the changes that are taking place. You are as responsible for the pregnancy as your wife is and should be as much a part of it as she is. By sharing as fully as possible in the experience, you will grow closer to her and your future baby and thus be an important factor in their health and physical welfare. We don't practice couvade, but researchers have found that women who have emotionally supportive partners adjust to their pregnancy more easily and enjoy it more than do women whose husbands remain aloof and do not get involved in the process. Your empathy and cool-headed support helps ease your wife's anxieties, and this carries over to the newborn infant. Relaxed women have easier births and give birth to babies who are calmer and less irritable than those born to highly anxious women.[2]

One thing that often calms pregnant women is seeing their fetus via ultrasound and finding out that it is normal and healthy. Most pregnant women now get sonograms, or ultrasound exams, which use sound waves to take pictures of the growing fetus. The images are used to tell if the fetus is growing at the normal rate, to determine sex, to predict the date of birth, and to detect such things as the possibility of twins or the existence of any possible life-threatening conditions. These tests are safer than X rays and appear to be free of hazards.[3]

Your wife already has direct physical contact with the fetus. If you are there when the first pictures of your baby are taken, you get to see your baby and begin the bonding, or attachment, process. Researchers have found that parents grow increasingly attached to the fetus during pregnancy, but seeing the fetus actually increases the rate of attachment for both mothers and fathers.[4]

Ultrasound tests also seem to be beneficial for pregnant moms and babies. Child psychologist Tiffany Field reports that seeing the fetus on an ultrasound screen can soothe a pregnant woman's anxieties and produce a healthier baby at birth. The women she tested seemed to enjoy the sight of the child's prebirth existence, and it calmed them. As their pregnancies progressed, they had less anxiety than did women who were tested but did not see the image of their fetus. In addition, they had fewer obstetric complications, and their infants weighed more at birth, scored higher on tests of alertness and responsiveness, and showed less irritability when handled.[5]

- Make sure that your baby's first nine months are spent in a safe and healthy environment—your wife's womb. If she smokes or drinks, the fetus can be harmed. If she takes drugs other than those prescribed by her obstetrician, the fetus can be harmed. Help her eat properly, get appropriate exercise and rest, and avoid emotional stress. Don't have wine with dinner in front of your pregnant wife. Give up things she has to avoid to make it easier for her to do so.
- Help your wife choose an obstetrician whom both of you trust and to whom you feel you can turn for information and guidance. Be sure the doctor recognizes the importance of your role as a true partner in the pregnancy and supports your participation.
- At the first sign of pregnancy, take your wife for a prenatal exam and schedule regular visits. Go with your wife to see the obstetrician, and don't just sit in the waiting room thumbing through back issues of magazines. There is less risk of misunderstandings or diagreements over medical restrictions if both of you talk regularly with the obstetrician. Keep notes on the

doctor's instructions, watch for symptoms of problems, and help your wife stick to her diet and sleep schedule.

- Be sure to go with your wife for her first ultrasound exam. "I fell in love with my baby when I saw it. I could actually see it move!" said one proud papa-to-be as he passed around a handful of Polaroid snaps of his three-month-old fetus.

- Talk to your fetus. Hold a rolled up newspaper to your wife's belly and let your baby begin to get used to your voice. Some research suggests that babys' brains are capable of some kinds of learning during the final months of pregnancy. But even if nothing happens, you will definitely be making contact with your wife.

- Set realistic limits and be firm about them. If your pregnant wife is overexerting herself, encourage her to take it easy. Help her finish what she is doing or do it for her. If visitors are tiring her, ask them to come back another time. Your wife may not realize how tired she is, but by being overly cautious, you can help her stay aware of her delicate condition.

- Find out as much as you can about pregnancy, and be prepared to deal with the changes you know are coming. Many woman have almost symptom-free pregnancies, but odd food cravings, heartburn, gas pains, frequent urination, and morning sickness are common during the early stages of pregnancy. Morning sickness may actually be good for your baby. It was once believed that a pregnant woman's nausea, vomiting, and illness at the sight of certain foods were caused by hormonal changes in her body. Recent findings suggest that morning sickness may be a way to protect the fetus. Foods that make pregnant women nauseated, such as coffee, tea, spices, bitter or strong-smelling vegetables, and less than fresh meat, contain chemicals that have little or no effect on adults but may have serious effects on the fetus. At least five studies have found that women who suffer vomiting or severe nausea during early pregnancy have lower rates of miscarriage than do those who have only mild sickness during pregnancy.[6]

- As the pregnancy progresses, your wife may become increasingly emotionally dependent, be irritable, and have sudden mood swings and bouts of depression. These are normal. Stay affectionately close to your wife. Be sensitive to her moods, and be prepared to deal sympathetically with them. It's all part of living with a pregnant woman. The pregnancy lasts only nine months, and any efforts you make will help your wife and the baby.

- Be patient with your pregnant wife, and most of all, don't let her get upset or stressed out. Stress effects hormone levels, which in turn effect the well-being of your fetus.

- Be aware of your partner's needs as well as her personality. Some women appreciate an expectant husband's protectiveness. Others see it as patronizing, condescending, and belittling. Do more than your share around the house, but don't undermine your wife's sense of competence. Let her know that her well-being and that of the baby are your primary concern, but don't treat her like an invalid.

- Go with your wife to exercise programs and childbirth training classes. These courses are not absolutely necessary, but you should attend them with your wife, especially if this is your first child.

- Plan to be present in the labor and delivery rooms. Most hospitals and doctors now allow this, and medical personnel are beginning to understand how important it is that you begin your fatherly role at childbirth.

More and more obstetricians permit and sometimes encourage expectant fathers to be present, even during cesarean births. If you are prepared and know what to expect, your calming presence will help your wife relax and have an easier delivery. You can rub her back, help her breathe properly, and time her contractions. The birth experience will be exciting and gratifying, something partners in pregnancy can look back on with pride as they become partners in parenting.

- Try not to be jealous of your growing fetus if your wife seems to be withdrawing from you. It is quite natural for her to turn inward and begin to focus more and more on the life inside her. Stay emotionally and physically close to her, and you will begin to develop similar feelings for your baby-to-be. If you feel that you are being replaced in your wife's affections by the ever-more-obvious fetus, discuss it with her. If it becomes a serious problem, seek help—but not in the arms of another woman.

PREGNANT SEX

Shapiro interviewed twenty-seven men who admitted to having had affairs while their wives were pregnant. In every case, he says, the affair severely damaged the marriage. The affairs also had several other things in common. Most of the men felt they needed someone to talk to about their feelings. Instead of confiding in their wives, they turned to other women. Often the other woman was someone close to the man's wife—a sister in one case, a mother in another—who was also feeling deserted because of the pregnancy. Most of these men had no history of affairs, and nearly all insisted that the wife's pregnant shape was not the reason for their infidelity. They simply felt left out.

The betraying men Shapiro talked to claimed that they continued to be sexually attracted to their pregnant wives, but that may have been their guilt speaking. Well-known sex researchers, Masters and Johnson, report that almost 40 percent of the men they interviewed gradually stopped making sexual advances to their wives during pregnancy, some because they were turned off by their wives' physical appearance. The remaining 60 percent said they continued to make sexual overtures throughout pregnancy, but some admitted to a decline in frequency. A few, however, said they wanted their wives even more during pregnancy. Some were turned on by pregnant women, and some wanted to get closer to their wives.[7]

Many of the pregnant women interviewed by Masters and Johnson claimed that their level of interest in sex was even higher during the first three months of pregnancy than it had been before they became pregnant. But most said their sexual drive and enjoyment of intercourse dropped off during the middle months of pregnancy.

Even though your sexual activity may slow during pregnancy, the quality of your relationship may depend on how you interact sexually. Your wife's nausea or tiredness might put a damper on sexual activity occasionally, but most couples can enjoy sex until quite late in the pregnancy. Your wife may have some strange sensations, such as spasms of the uterus when she has an orgasm, but these are usually harmless and no cause for alarm. Your wife may be uncomfortable making love during the later stages of pregnancy, but many women say they are surprised at how sexually responsive they are during this period.

- Compliment your pregnant partner by continuing to show sexual interest in her. If you do feel inhibited, discuss your concerns with her and explain your reactions. If you don't feel as sexually stimulated by your wife as you did before she was pregnant, try different positions or surroundings that might arouse your sexual interest.
- Don't let fear of hurting your pregnant wife or the fetus dampen your desire for sex. Normal sexual activity is quite safe for both. During the final months of pregnancy it is probably best to avoid extremely vigorous intercourse, particularly when the position puts pressure on your wife's abdomen, but you can find positions that are comfortable for her or engage in sexual activities that do not involve intercourse.
- If your sexual activity does decline during pregnancy, for whatever reason, do not let it interfere with the quality of your relationship. Whether you have sex once a day or once a week or even if you agree to avoid sex during pregnancy, the important issue is that both partners continue to feel positive and supportive of each other. Feeling pressured, martyred, or abused about sexual activity during pregnancy or any other time is not the best way to maintain a healthy relationship.

I DON'T WANT ANOTHER BROTHER OR SISTER!

Your pregnant wife has all the physical signs she needs to help her get into the mother mode. You may have to put a little more effort into preparing yourself, and if you already have children, they may have an even more difficult time getting ready for what is about to take place. Their three- or four-person world is about to change with the arrival of a new baby, and there is a good chance that jealousy will rear its ugly head. But if you are a close and loving father, you can help keep sibling rivalry to a minimum. If you are close to your older children, they may be willing to discuss their fears and jealousy with you. Your pregnant wife may withdraw some of her emotional support from your older children as the big day nears, but if you tighten your bonds with them as well as show them you are happy about the new baby, you may be able to calm their fears about sharing their world.

- Encourage your older children to get involved in preparations for the new baby. Invite them to help paint the nursery and fix up the baby's crib. Give them a preview of what the baby will be like by showing them pictures of themselves as newborns. Go shopping and let the older children help pick out clothes for the new baby. This gets them involved and gives them a sense of family responsibility.
- Be careful of focusing too much on the new baby. It can be very upsetting to a child's sense of security to have everything seem to revolve around the new baby. Encourage your friends and relatives not to ignore your older children. And make sure that you and your wife each set aside special times for each child before and after the arrival of the new baby.
- Examine your own feelings about being an only child or about relationships you may have had with any brothers or sisters. Remember that the way you treat your children may be related to your own childhood and how you were treated by your parents or brothers and sisters. Also, consider your wife's birth-order position.

HOME FROM THE HOSPITAL

After several false alarms and unnecessary trips to the hospital, Julie finally went into what turned out to be a twenty-three-hour labor and gave birth to her first son. Less than twenty-four hours later, while she was getting the first real rest she had had in almost a week, the head nurse came into her hospital room and told her it was time to get packing, time to go home. Julie was shocked. She was tired, she could barely walk, and she hadn't even fed her infant yet. And that's the way it is in more and more hospitals.

Thirty years ago, a new mother might have recovered in the hospital for a week or two. She would have been completely healed, would have received training in infant care, and would have been given help with breast-feeding. Now, with typical maternity ward charges running about $500 a day, some insurance companies are limiting hospital stays to a day or two unless there are medical complications. Two weeks may have been excessive, but one day doesn't give the mother, the baby, or the father much time to prepare for the new world they are entering.

One of the first challenges they face is depression. More than half of all new mothers have episodes of crying and sadness during the first ten days after giving birth. Hormonal changes and fatigue contribute to postpartum depression, but it is only natural to have some letdown after the exhilaration and relief of giving birth. For many women the depression is mild and short-lived, quickly replaced by her pride and joy in being a new mother. For others, it can be longer lasting. The physical stresses of childbirth, the pressures of being a new mother or of having an infant who is difficult to soothe, possible feelings of neglect by her husband—all of these concerns can increase the risk of a woman suffering from serious postpartum depression.

One of your jobs as a father is to keep your wife's depression to a minimum. If your new baby is temperamental or cranky, you will have to be especially supportive. When researchers measured women's moods three to six months before and three months after their babies were born, they found that the women most likely to have serious postpartum depression were those who had difficult babies. Their infants cried a lot for long periods of time and did not respond well to attempts to soothe them. The researchers suggest that the link between the baby's temperament and the mother's depression may be related to the mother's feelings about herself. If she has trouble comforting her baby, she begins to feel incompetent as a mother. She may become ambivalent about the baby, causing guilt and even lower self-esteem. There's not much you can do about a baby's inborn temperament, but you can help lower your wife's level of stress and depression by being highly supportive. The women who had the most support from their husbands felt more confident as mothers and felt less depressed.[8]

- When you bring your new family home from the hospital, remember that your wife has just been through an emotional and physical adventure that has drained her. She needs all the support—physical and emotional—you can give. The more you help her, the less likely she is to have severe postpartum depression.
- Take paternity leave, vacation, or sick time to be with your new family as much as possible. No matter how many children you have, each addition means that new relationships have to be made, and you should be in on them from the start.

- Reward your wife for what she has just given you. Make her comfortable, especially during the first days home from the hospital. Wash the dishes, clean the house, help her care for the baby. If you weren't doing your share of the household work before the baby was born, this is a good time to start. Give your wife everything she needs and deserves, and don't go around acting put upon or like you are some kind of superdad. You will only be doing what every man should be more than willing to do for his wife and new child.

- Be careful you don't give your wife more than she needs, and don't make her feel that you are trying to outdo her as a parent. One woman thought she was lucky because her husband took care of the baby and did all the shopping, cooking, washing, ironing, and cleaning. She divorced him, saying that he made her feel useless.[9]

- Your wife needs to know how important she is as a mother, wife, and person. She may, for instance, be concerned that she is losing her attractiveness or her career or that she isn't a competent mother. She may even show occasional signs of resentment toward the baby, who is now getting all the attention. Help her avoid these feelings by showing that you are as committed to her as to the new baby. Help her maintain her sense of individuality and self-confidence. Encourage her to get back into doing the things you know she likes to do.

- The birth of a child, especially your first one, will challenge your relationship with your wife. Old patterns will be gone. New ones will have to be formed. Work closely with your wife to fit your new baby comfortably into your life-style, and try to maintain or recapture the level of closeness you had prior to the birth of the baby. Don't just sit back and accept whatever kind of family relationship evolves. Get involved, stay involved, and decide with your wife what you want your new family to be.

- Work closely with your wife to make parenthood a sharing, cooperative experience. Remember that you are as responsible for the new baby as she is. Your wife probably knows a lot more about how to take care of babies than you do, so ask her to give you some practical tips. As long as she realizes that you may have some good ideas of your own, having her coach you is an excellent way to get you involved in your new responsibilities, especially as they evolve. It also lets your wife know that you are serious about being a father and want to do your fair share.

- Some couples can afford to hire help after the baby arrives. If you can, don't hire someone to take care of the baby and let your wife do the housework. Hire someone to do the housework. Don't take on extra work so you can hire a housekeeper. Do the housework yourself, and spend as much time as possible at home with your wife and new baby.

- Be prepared for some of your friends to treat you differently. Unmarried friends or couples without children may feel uncomfortable around new parents. Some may be jealous or resent the intrusion of a child. They may not be interested in your vast collection of baby pictures. Be careful not to get so wrapped up in fatherhood that you forget your friends. Give them time to adjust to the situation. They will. Try to welcome them into your new family life, but don't feel that you have to accept every invitation in order to keep your friends. If you have to miss a party or a ball game, most of your friends will understand.

- Be ready and willing to give up a lot of your freedom in order to take care of the baby, but don't give up everything. It may not seem worth the hassle to find a baby-sitter so you can go out with your wife once in a while, but it is important that you maintain some of your preparenting activities. It is also important that both of you get back into some of your individual interests. Take turns caring for the baby in the evenings so that each of you gets time to go out. Your wife may begin to feel trapped if you don't share in parenting.

- If your wife wants to breast-feed your new baby, support her decision. She needs to be comfortable and confident to breast-feed successfully, and you can help her by being encouraging and supportive. If you pressure your wife to get back to all of her regular activities as soon as possible after giving birth, you will interfere with her ability to effectively feed your baby.

- Don't let breast-feeding become a major focus of family life, and don't get left out of the process. You will never be able to feed the baby the way your wife does, but you are just as important to your child as she is and should spend as much time with your baby as she does. Use a breast pump occasionally to bottle-feed your baby. This will keep you involved and take some of the pressure off your wife. It will give her more free time during the day and more sleep at night when the baby wakes up hungry.

- If your wife can't or doesn't want to breast-feed your baby, support her. The quality of your interactions with your wife and your child are much more important than how the baby gets fed.

BUT I WANTED A BOY

You are less likely to get divorced if your first child is a boy rather than a girl. If you have two boys, you are less likely to divorce than if you have a boy and a girl or two girls. When sociologist S. Philip Morgan uncovered these disturbing facts in U.S. census data, he thought it might have something to do with the way men relate to their sons. Morgan and his colleagues looked at findings from a Temple University survey of parents and children and found that although women feel close to both sons and daughters, men feel closer to sons than daughters. They get more involved in the daily lives of their sons and spend more time with them. The children confirmed this. Sons reported spending more quality time with their fathers than did daughters. And society reinforces this. A man is much more likely to play ball with his son than to help his daughter pick out a doll. Why would this make marriages more stable? Morgan says that men's tendency to be more closely involved in the lives of their sons than their daughters increases their commitment to family life and decreases the chances of divorce.[10]

Morgan's findings are disturbing because they indicate that men still favor males over females, which is probably true for society in general. Morgan's findings may be troubling, but they are not surprising. Throughout history, men have wanted sons for narcissistic reasons. Many still want their first child to be a boy or want to keep having children until they have a little man to follow in their footsteps. Some women also want to have sons because they know that men have an advantage in a society that still devalues women. And it all starts with the sexist attitudes we hold and pass on to our children. That may be the way things are, but it is not the way they have to be.

- Don't be disappointed in the sex of your child. Remember that individual differences are far more important than sex differences and that the sex of your child is not as important as the fact that he or she develops a high level of self-esteem and becomes a happy, successful adult.

- Play with your infant daughter as eagerly and actively as you would with a son. Researchers consistently point out that fathers treat boys and girls differently. While playing, they look at and touch their sons more often than they do their daughters. They give their sons more visual stimulation by showing them toys more often than they do their daughters.[11] If you follow this pattern, you may be shortchanging your daughter, who needs your attention as much as your son does. (See Chapter 4 for more on how your attitudes and behavior influence the development of your sons and daughters.)

- Accept each child for his or her unique qualities, and any initial disappointment you may have felt will disappear as you grow closer and help your child become the best that he or she can be. Whether a child is male or female, slim or muscular, intellectually brilliant or below average, timid or extremely assertive, he or she needs your interest, understanding, support, and love.

REFERENCES

1. Shapiro, J., The Expectant Father, *Psychology Today*, January 1987, p. 36.

2. Grossman, F., et al., "Fathers and Children: Predicting the Quality and Quantity of Fathering" *Developmental Psychology*, Vol. 24, 1988, p. 82.

3. Fackelmann, K., How Safe Is a Sonogram? *Science News*, April 4, 1992, p. 218.

4. Eichmann, M., Yusim, V., and Zuskar, D., "Fetal Sex Identification and Components of Attachment" paper presented at meeting of the American Psychological Association, San Francisco, August 1991.

5. Py-Liberman, B., Mom, Meet Your Baby, *Psychology Today*, June 1989, p. 18.

6. Morning Sickness Good for Baby, *Science*, Vol. 257, August 7, 1992, p. 743.

7. Masters, W., and Johnson, V., *Human Sexual Response*. Boston: Little, Brown, 1966.

8. Cutrona, C., and Troutman, B., "Social Support, Infant Treatment, and Parenting Self-Efficacy" *Child Development*, Vol. 55, 1986, p. 1507.

9. Tarvis, C., Divorcing the Perfect Husband, *Psychology Today*, March 1983, p. 73.

10. Adessa, M. "Divorce Insurance: Have a Son," *Psychology Today*, May, 1988, p. 14.

11. Parke, R. *Fathers*. Cambridge, MA: Harvard University Press, 1981.

SUGGESTED READINGS

WHEN PARTNERS BECOME PARENTS: THE BIG LIFE CHANGE FOR COUPLES by Cowan, C. and Cowan, P., Basic Books, 1992.

SOONER OR LATER: THE TIMING OF PARENTING IN ADULT LIVES by Daniels, P., and Weingarten, K., Norton, 1982.

WHEN MEN ARE PREGNANT: NEEDS AND CONCERNS OF EXPECTANT FATHERS by Shapiro, J., Delta, 1993.

The Father-Baby Bond

Joe was only eighteen hours old when he watched his first basketball game with his dad. They were in the hospital the morning after Joe was born, and the happy dad was oohing and aahing, marveling at his son's delicate little toenails and saying things like "Look! He's smiling at me. He knows me." When friends and relatives started visiting and giving Mom and the new baby all the attention, Dad turned on the television to check out a Saturday afternoon basketball game. Later, after everyone had left and Mom wanted to take a nap, it was Dad's turn to monopolize Joe for a while. He lifted his son gently, kissed him on the top of his bald little head, and, after a few minutes, turned him around to face the TV. Dad didn't really expect Joe to watch the game. He wasn't even sure the baby could see what was on the screen, but he was doing something he liked doing, and he was thrilled to be doing it with his new son.

Joe's father may not have realized it, but he was already beginning to teach his son not about basketball, but about the differences between moms and dads. Mom takes the intimate approach. She holds Joe close to her breast, stares long and lovingly into his eyes, and whispers sweet nothings in his ear. Dad holds Joe securely in his lap but turns him around to face the world and bounces him and makes loud noises when someone scores a basket. Yes, even in the first days of life, Joe and any other baby boy or girl is capable of learning about and responding to these and the many subtle and not so subtle differences between mothers and fathers.

Not too many years ago, most people thought babies were born blind; that they couldn't taste, smell, or feel pain; and that there was nothing but a blooming, buzzing confusion inside their tiny unformed brains. Then, in the 1960s, a technology explosion gave child psychologists the tools they needed to examine and interpret the highly complex behaviors of babies. Soon, infants replaced white rats as the psychologist's favorite object of study. Videocameras and monitors let them examine and reexamine elusive gestures and expressions, and other high-tech equipment allowed them to monitor respiration, heart rate, body movement, eye movements, and sucking behavior—all of which give reliable clues to what is going on inside the infant.

Most parents now know that babies do more than eat, sleep, and dirty their diapers. They are fabulous little creatures with a wide range of amazing abilities. By the time they are three or four days old, they can recognize your smell, voice, and face. Within hours of birth, they can respond to and imitate your facial expressions. Try sticking your tongue out at a baby. If the child is healthy and alert, you'll probably get a tongue right back at you. Facial imitation is among the baby's first attempts at communication and a good indication that newborns play an active role in their world right from the start. They are interested in, even fascinated by, the people around them. They don't just lie there and wait for you to feed them or play with them. They use their smiles, cries, and movements to get your attention, to get you to love, nurture, and stimulate them. They are programmed to learn, and they want you to teach them.

Babies aren't the only ones whose abilities have been underestimated. Many parents still think there is some kind of maternal instinct, that women—but not men— have an inborn sensitivity to infants. It then follows wrongly that mothers should be the primary parent during a child's first years of life. Many fathers even doubt their own ability to deal with the needs of a newborn and wistfully look forward to getting more actively involved when the child is older. But these notions are wrong. What we used to call the *maternal* instinct is actually a *parental* instinct because both parents can become thoroughly attached to their infants and can be sensitive and nurturing toward them. There is no biological imperative that makes the mother-infant bond more important than the father-infant bond.

For instance, fathers who have the opportunity to see, hold, and react to their infants within twenty-four hours of their birth tend to be just like mothers, experiencing feelings of enthrallment and bonding.[1] Like mothers, they develop an intense feeling of attachment and intimacy. Fathers are usually fascinated by even the smallest details of their child's appearance and movements and become preoccupied with and intensely absorbed in the baby. And these feelings show up in the way new fathers behave. They stare into the baby's big eyes and count the tiny toes. They touch, hold, kiss, explore, and imitate the infant as often as mothers do. The only thing mothers do more often than fathers is smile at their babies.[2] And when fathers, for one reason or another, take over primary responsibility for their infants, they are just as sensitive to infant behavior and as competent in nurturing babies as are mothers.

There has been a tendency to keep fathers in the background during the first year or so of an infant's life, but there is no reason to do so. Men have always been capable of nurturing babies and of developing strong bonds of attachment to them. Happily enough, infants can then become attached to their fathers as securely as to their mothers. When babies are born, they have no real preference for one parent over the other or for a natural over an adoptive or foster parent. They simply like to be held and stimulated and don't seem to care who the holder is as long as that person is sensitive to their needs. At this stage, infants can become attached to any person who is a consistent source of comfort, attention, and stimulation. In general, however, many more mothers than fathers are regularly involved with infant care, and most babies do develop a primary bond with their mother rather than their father. But they also form other attachments, and observations of close-knit families indicate that during the first year of life babies become just as interested in their fathers as in their mothers.[3]

How can you bond deeply and naturally with your newborn?

■ Get bonded to your baby as soon as possible. Try giving the baby a massage. Infants, like all of us, love to be touched and caressed by gentle hands. Imagine how you would feel if you were cooped up in a crib all day and couldn't get any exercise. By massaging your baby, you strengthen the physical bond that is developing between you and promote not only physical but social and cognitive growth. Premature infants usually lag behind full-term infants in all areas of development, but researchers have shown that preemies who are massaged for five minutes twice a day catch up much more quickly than those who do not get this kind of physical and social stimulation, and those with highly involved fathers are the ones who do the best.[4]

- Don't let your wife be the one who jumps every time the baby cries. Taking care of your child's needs is one of the most natural ways to strengthen the father-infant bond. Feeding, bathing, changing, and dressing the baby provide excellent opportunities for you to learn about each other. And since you and the mother are likely to have different styles, even when doing the same thing, you will be exposing your baby to a broader range of stimulation. At first, you may not be as patient or adept as the baby's mother and you may not like the idea of getting up in the middle of the night to feed or change your baby. But remember that sharing child-care responsibilities strengthens your relationship with the baby's mother as well as with your infant.

- Carry your baby around with you as much as possible. This may be especially helpful if you have a colicky infant that cries a lot. It seems that babies cry less in societies where mothers carry them around with them for long periods of time. When researchers tested this out, they found that carrying does stop crying. They studied ninety-nine families with infants between three and twelve weeks of age. Half the parents were told to carry their babies in their arms or in carriers for a minimum of three hours every day—not only when the baby cried and whether the baby was awake or asleep. The other parents were given mobiles and pictures of faces to put in their babies' cribs. The parents kept diaries and recorded the amount of time their infants spent asleep and awake and whether they were content, fussing, feeding, or crying. The more parents carried their infants, the less the babies cried and the more content they seemed to be. An average increase of two hours carrying time was associated with a 42 percent decrease in crying and fussing. The researchers aren't sure why extra carrying reduces crying, but they suggest that it may be a more effective way to handle crying problems than simply putting a bottle in your baby's mouth.[5]

- If carrying your baby around doesn't help, try taking the baby for a drive. Getting out of the house and going for a ride might be relaxing and calming for both of you.

- Don't expect your baby to be silent no matter how much carrying or driving you do. Crying is your baby's first language, and they use it to tell you they are hungry or uncomfortable or simply need some attention. Even during their first twenty-four hours of life, infants make different crying sounds when they are being held, bathed, or fed, and you will quickly learn to distinguish these cries. Almost all mothers and 84 percent of fathers can distinguish the cries of their own babies from those of other infants. "It is the sound of the cry that parents listen to to determine what the infant needs," explains psychologist Barry Lester. "Parents tune in to this channel, learn to understand what their infant is trying to say . . . and establish the foundation of a communication system." Your newborn won't make any noises that sound like speech for the first three or four months, but crying is practice for the words soon to come. It helps infants become aware of their lips, tongue, palate, jaw, and voice, explains speech pathologist Thomas Murry. As they grow older, their cries shorten and begin to approach the length of syllables and words and become almost speechlike in terms of rate and rhythm by nine months. By about the time of their first birthday, they begin to echo back the sounds you have been filling their ears with.[6]

- Take advantage of your baby's learning abilities by being a regular source of stimulation. Spend as much time as possible with your wife and newborn baby, but make sure you try to reserve at least sixty minutes each day for one-on-one activities with your child, whether it be feeding, washing, and caring for your baby or reading to, playing with, tickling, and just holding your baby.

- Keep a diary of how much time you spend with your infant every day and what you do during that time. Make sure that your "quality time" really is quality time—reading to, talking to, playing with your baby— whatever the two of you can do together that makes you both happy.

- Smile at your baby. If your baby is almost three months old or older, you will be rewarded with a smile. The smile, along with eye contact, is one of the first signs of attachment between you and your baby. The warm feeling you get when your baby smiles back at you helps tighten the father-baby bond. Infants not only imitate your facial expressions, they imitate your moods. Babies who are reared by constantly depressed parents tend to be moody and to frown, cry, and fuss more than other babies. And it can be a vicious cycle. Such babies may get less attention from their parents, which can interfere with their normal intellectual and social development.

- Talk to your baby. Don't be embarrassed to sing or croon or make funny noises. Holding a baby in your arms will mellow you and make it easier for you to express your emotions. And this may well carry over to your relationship with your wife and strengthen your marriage. Most surveys indicate that women want their husbands to talk to them more, to express their emotions.

- Don't just talk nonsense to your baby. Tell your baby stories. Talk about what you do at work. Even though the baby won't have the faintest idea what you are talking about, you will be laying the foundation for the development of communication skills. You will be teaching the baby how to make eye contact and about the up and down, give and take of normal conversation. But don't do all the talking. Go back and forth with the baby. Encourage the baby to babble and make noises in between your statements and help your infant begin to understand that conversation is a two-way street. If you do all the talking, the baby doesn't get a chance to practice. Help your baby learn to speak by acknowledging his or her attempts to communicate even when the attempts are incomprehensible. As the sounds become words, encourage your baby to talk more. If your baby says "I want my blanket," respond by saying "Your blanket?" or "This blanket?" or "The blue blanket?" This gives the baby a chance to say yes or no and join in the conversation.

- Watch how your baby reacts to and learns from new situations. Hang a mobile over the baby's crib and tie a ribbon from the mobile to one of your baby's arms or legs. Even a six-week-old will learn very quickly how to make the mobile move. If you take the mobile down, then replace it two weeks later, your baby will probably remember which arm or leg to move even if it is not attached to the mobile.[7] Such early signs of memory are the basis for the kinds of learning from experience that go on throughout life. Don't forget to untie your baby when you leave the room.

- The more you know about the abilities of your baby, the more likely you will be to stimulate and encourage those abilities. Use the Brazelton Neonatal Assessment Scale that child specialists and pediatricians use to monitor various aspects of infant development. This will make you more aware of the abilities of your infant, encourage you to pay more attention to your child and provide the stimulation and interaction that promotes physical, social, and mental development. Rate yourself and your baby once a week. When one group of parents did this, their infants scored higher than average on a test of intellectual abilities one year later.[4]

DADS ARE DIFFERENT

Being bonded to two loving parents offers babies special advantages because Dad and Mom provide two different people to learn about as well as separate but special sources of love and support. Babies quickly learn, for example, that Mom and Dad can be expected to fulfill different needs. If, as in most families, Mom is the primary caretaker and feeds the baby, a hungry or tired baby will probably reach out to her for comfort and care. A baby who is bored and ready for a little action will usually look for Dad, who is more likely than Mom to get the child involved in some kind of vigorous play or stimulating activity.

When you play with your baby he or she is often
1. *sleepy*
2. *alert*
3. *upset*

How much do you have to stimulate your baby to get him or her to look at you?
1. *not very much*
2. *a fair amount*
3. *a lot*

When your baby is upset what does he or she do to quiet himself or herself?
1. *brings hand to mouth*
2. *sucks with nothing in his or her mouth*
3. *looks at you*

Try talking to your baby holding your face about one foot away from his or her face and then slowly move your face to one side and then to the other as you continue talking. When you do this your baby
1. *doesn't look at you*
2. *becomes quiet and looks at you*
3. *follows your face to each side with his or her head and eyes*
4. *follows your face with his or her head and eyes, up and down and to each side*

Now try the same thing, only move your face without talking. When you do this your baby
1. *doesn't look at you*
2. *becomes quiet*
3. *follows your face with head and eyes*
4. *follows your face with his or her head and eyes, up and down and to each side*

Try talking to your baby from one side of his or her head and then from the other. When you do this he or she
1. *has no reaction or blinks*
2. *becomes quiet*

3. *turns eyes and head to your voice once or twice*
4. *turns eyes and head to your voice more than two times*

Now try holding a colorful toy or some shiny object in front of your baby's face and then move it slowly to each side of his or her head and then up and down. When you do this he or she

1. *doesn't look at the toy*
2. *becomes quiet and looks at toy*
3. *follows the toy you are moving with head and eyes*
4. *follows the toy you are moving with head and eyes, up and down and to each side*

Try shaking a rattle on one side of your baby's head and then on the other side. When you do this he or she

1. *has no reaction or blinks*
2. *becomes quiet*
3. *turns eyes and head to the rattle once or twice*
4. *turns eyes and head to the rattle more than two times*

When you did the above things with your baby he or she usually

1. *paid little attention to you or the toy*
2. *had short periods of watching you or the toy*
3. *watched for a fairly long time*
4. *paid attention most of the time*

How does your baby feel when you handle or hold him or her?

1. *limp like a rag doll*
2. *limp some of time*
3. *relaxed but firm*
4. *very tense*

When your baby moves his or her arms the movements are

1. *jerky most of the time*
2. *jerky some of the time*

3. *smooth some of the time*
4. *smooth most of the time*

When you pick up your baby and hold him or her in a rocking position he or she
1. *often swings his or her arms and kicks his or her legs and squirms a lot*
2. *is like a sack of meal in your arms*
3. *relaxes and nestles his or her head in the crook of your arms*
4. *moves his or her face toward you and reaches out to grab your clothing*

When your baby is crying very hard
1. *nothing seems to quiet him or her*
2. *only a pacifier will quiet him or her*
3. *holding and rocking will quiet him or her*
4. *talking and holding your hand on his or her stomach quiets him or her*

Please circle those activities that upset your baby
1. *changing his or her diaper*
2. *undressing or dressing him or her*
3. *putting him or her back in the bassinet*
4. *lying him or her on his or her stomach*

How often does your baby tremble when he or she is warmly dressed?
1. *not very often*
2. *occasionally*
3. *fairly often*
4. *very often*

When your baby is crying, how successful is he or she at quieting himself or herself?
1. *cannot quiet himself or herself*
2. *makes several attempts to quiet himself or herself but is usually unsuccessful*
3. *has many brief successes at quieting himself or herself*

4. *often quiets himself or herself for long periods of time*

How would you describe your baby's hand-to-mouth activity?

1. *makes no attempt to bring his or her hands to his or her mouth*

2. *often brings a hand next to his or her mouth*

3. *sometimes puts his or her fist or fingers in his or her mouth*

4. *sometimes sucks on fist or fingers for as long as 15 seconds at a time*

How many times has your baby looked like he or she was smiling at you?

Even if fathers and mothers behave in generally similar ways toward the baby, they produce contrasting images that can be quite pleasing and exciting to an infant. Dad is usually larger than Mom, with a deeper voice and different clothes. He also moves and reacts differently, smells and feels different. In addition to having distinctive sounding voices, mothers and fathers tend to use different verbal styles when talking to their infants, and these differences are an important source of stimulation and learning because even very young infants listen to what they hear and try to imitate it. And what they learn from you will probably be different from what they learn from your wife because of the typical differences between male and female brains.[8] Mom's brain may be better at verbal and personal skills. Yours may be better at spatial skills and makes you behave more competitively. By being closely involved with your children, you give them a chance to learn about the male way of seeing and reacting to the world. For example, you probably have better mechanical abilities than your wife and can help develop similar skills in your children. Your wife is probably better at interpersonal and communication skills and can foster those abilities in your children. By working together as partners in parenting, you ensure that your children get the best of both brains.

The differences in the daily schedules of mothers and fathers can also be important to the baby. Because many mothers stay home with their very young infants while fathers are usually at work during the day, a father's (or mother's) comings and goings can be very stimulating to an infant. When Mom excitedly declares "Daddy's home!" or "Daddy's coming home in just a few minutes!" it increases the baby's awareness of events being linked in sequence and helps the baby begin to realize the regularity of Dad's comings and goings and his importance in the family. Of course, you can do the same with respect to your wife's comings and goings.

Infants and young babies who are closely bonded to a parent show signs of what is called *separation anxiety* when that parent leaves the room. They fuss and cry. But no parent can be available twenty-four hours a day; work and other commitments make separation unavoidable. A secure attachment to two parents, however, generally makes it much easier for a child to accept limited periods of separation from either parent. Researchers study separation anxiety by watching how a child reacts when various combinations of the mother, the father, and a stranger enter and leave a room in which the child is playing. Most one-year-old children don't get too upset when one or the other parent leaves the room. But almost all babies cry and show signs of distress when both parents leave and they are alone with the stranger. Children with highly involved fathers, however, show the least amount of crying and anxiety while those with less involved fathers tend to become very disturbed when left with the stranger. The extra love and attention from having two involved parents seems to give the child a sense of security, a sort of protection against fearfulness, even in strange situations.

Differences between the father's and mother's activities also offer great learning opportunities for babies. Infants have a remarkable ability to soak up knowledge of the world. As long as their basic needs are met, the more experiences, sights, sounds, smells, and tastes they are exposed to, the more they learn. Even if the baby doesn't understand what is going on, seeing, hearing, touching, and feeling new things in the company of a trusted and loving father will be a positively exciting experience.

- Take your baby with you whenever possible and practical. There is usually no reason why the baby can't be taken along on all kinds of outings, routine errands, as well as more special trips. Use your imagination. Take your baby to a restaurant. You can always get up and take the baby for a walk if he or she begins to cry and disturb the other customers. Take your baby to visit friends and relatives, especially if there are other children to play with.
- Constant exposure to a wide range of experiences and people helps infants become more adaptable so that they are less of a problem with each outing. Some children are, of course, more naturally outgoing than others. So have contingency plans if your child is not happy in certain situations. Bring along toys your baby likes and whatever else you need to change any environment into one that meets your baby's needs. Fi-

nally, keep your baby's and your own temperament in mind when you plan excursions. A difficult baby and a father who runs out of patience easily are not a good combination for happy outings. Neither are dads who do not carefully monitor their baby's behavior in other people's homes.

- If your job requires travel, consider taking your baby with you. If that isn't practical, try not to be away from your infant for more than two or three days at a time. Even a brief separation from a loved parent can be extremely upsetting to infants who have a limited sense of time and who will not realize that the separation is only temporary. If possible, try to hold off lengthy trips away from your family until the child is at least two or three years old. Children are usually much better able to handle long separations after the age of two, when they have developed some sense of the permanency and continuity of relationships.

BOYS AND GIRLS ARE DIFFERENT

Kevin lost his penis when he was seven months old. It was an accident, but a serious one. He and his identical twin brother, Ken, were brought in to be circumcised with an electric cauterizing instrument. When it was Kevin's turn, the instrument overheated and severely burned the entire tissue of his penis, which eventually decayed and fell off.

The names have been changed, but the story is true. Although it can never have a completely happy ending, the story is by no means a tragedy. Kevin became Karen, and by the age of six, she was living the life of a healthy, almost normal girl.[9] The parents were very farsighted. Ten months after the accident, realizing how cruel it would be to rear one twin boy with and one without a penis, they agreed to a sex reassignment for Kevin. When he was seventeen months old, they changed his name, clothes, and hairstyle. Four months later, the first step of genital reconstruction as a female was taken. The parents got advice and counseling on how to raise Karen and treated him as a girl in all ways. Before long, their efforts began to show, with Karen imitating her mother and Ken, his father. Karen wanted and got dolls and a doll house one Christmas. Ken asked for and got a toy garage with cars and gas pumps. Karen said she wanted to grow up to be a doctor or a teacher. Ken wanted to be a fireman or policeman. As they grew older, Karen became more and more feminine, and Ken actually grew taller than his identical twin.

You won't be changing the sex of your children as these parents did, but you will be shaping them just as profoundly. From the moment you learn the sex of your child, you—and the rest of the world—will treat him or her differently. But long before you trot out the pink or blue, nature will have directed your infant's path toward masculinity or femininity. It begins when your sperm, with either an X (female) or Y (male) chromosome, fertilizes your wife's egg. For the next six weeks, male and female fetuses look exactly the same. But then either male or female genitals begin to develop and produce either male or female hormones, which influence the way the brain will grow from then on. And the brain and hormones will influence your child's behavior for the rest of his or her life. A male brain and hormones will tend to make your son more aggressive and give him better visual–spatial and mathematical abilities than most little girls. A female brain and hormones will tend to make your daughter more physically and emotionally sensitive and give her better verbal abilities than most little boys.

Twenty years ago many people were skeptical of such findings, saying that society's sexist ways, not biology, forced little boys and girls in different directions. That's true, but the evidence continues to pile up indicating that male and female brains are different even before birth and continue to be different. Karen's parents taught her to be a girl, but they couldn't change her masculine brain. Karen became feminine in most ways, but she was also an aggressive, tomboyish little girl.

"Male and female brains differ. That's a given," says Christina Williams, head of the psychology department at Barnard College. Male and female brains may have different strengths, she argues, but they are both perfect. "It's like the difference between a Macintosh and an IBM computer".[10] Brain researcher Marian Diamond agrees. "Men and women," she says, "will have more tolerance for each other as we learn more about our brain similarities and differences".[11]

Once researchers began to take seriously the possibility that male and female brains are different, the exact nature of those differences and their subtle effects on the way men and women, boys and girls, think and behave began to become clear. At birth, however, the differences are minimal. It is how we respond to them that makes the real difference in how our children grow. As the case of Karen and Ken demonstrates, there are ways to get around Mother Nature. We can try to teach little boys how to channel their aggressive tendencies in positive directions. We can give them special help if they have reading problems. We can try to teach little girls to be more self-confident and assertive. We can give them special help if they have problems with math. Infants may have male or female brains, but those brains still have a long time to grow. And as they grow, new connections continue to be made. You as a father will have a great deal to do with the development of your child's brain.

But this is not a one-way street. Your baby will ask for and get special kinds of treatment that reinforce his or her inborn tendencies. Most infant girls, for example, are more responsive to touch and sound than are boys, and you will probably find yourself treating a girl more gently and talking to her more softly than you would a boy. Most infant boys are more active than girls and will smile and let you know that they like you to play a little more roughly with them. And when you talk more to girls or play more roughly with boys, you exaggerate what were originally minor sex differences.

By the time of your baby's first birthday, both inborn and socially influenced sex differences will be even more obvious. Little girls tend to talk earlier than boys and seem to pay more attention to your facial expressions and what you say to them. Boys venture farther from their parents, stay away from them longer, and look at them less than do girls. Boys also tend to be more aggressive. When researchers place a barrier between an infant boy and his parents, he will try to crawl around it to get back to Mommy or Daddy. A little girl is more likely to stay put and cry in frustration.

As sex differences continue to emerge, it appears that fathers are more likely than mothers to encourage them. Most mothers treat their newborn boys and girls the same; they spend a lot of time soothing them and trying to keep them calm and comfortable. Fathers are more likely to gently cuddle infant daughters but be playful and encourage more rough-and-tumble play with boys. Many fathers treat girls as if they are too delicate and fragile to handle. Fathers are more likely than mothers to encourage their infant sons to move faster, crawl further, or reach higher and are usually less concerned than mothers about the baby getting tired or dirty.

Fathers are also more apt to accept a temperamentally difficult baby boy but to withdraw from a fussy girl. Some of these differences are due to traditional sexist attitudes on the part of men, but babies also play a role. Fathers may pay more attention to infant boys than girls because most baby boys appear to be happier than girls with Dad's rough-and-tumble play. More baby girls than boys react negatively to high-intensity physical stimulation, preferring Mom's gentle touch.

The question of sexism in the nursery has been debated for more than twenty years now, and there is no doubt that highly rigid sex-role expectations can be damaging. But even the most liberated parents who have done everything they can think of to keep sexist attitudes out of their families will probably find that their boys still want to play with trucks; their girls, with dolls. In fact, most young children go through a rather rigid stage of sex typing even when both parents are strong believers in nonsexist child rearing. Children learn the difference between fathers and mothers and form a clear image of themselves as either male or female. Walk into almost any day-care center full of two- and three-year-olds and you will probably see most of the boys playing with boys, doing boy things. The girls will have their own group and attitudes and activities. At this age, young children have a much more simplistic view of the world than do adults or even older boys and girls. Once they discover that they belong to the category of male or female, they naturally want to be like older, bigger people of the same sex. In fact, developmental psychologists Lawrence Kohlberg and Edward Zigler have found that very bright preschoolers are apt to be more rigidly sex-typed at three or four years of age than are their less intellectually gifted playmates. However, as they grow older, the brightest children show more sex-role flexibility than other children.[12] They appear to be less constrained by sexual stereotypes and have the sense of security and confidence to express their individual interests by the time they reach fourth or fifth grade.

- Promote positive gender development in your children by being an involved father. Your son will have what it takes to become a man, but you have to show him what kind of man to be. The same goes for your daughter. Work with your wife, and share in all areas of child rearing. You will be showing your children from the time they are born the best of the masculine and feminine worlds and how these worlds compliment each other. In far too many families, Mom is left to make all the day-to-day decisions involving the children while good old Dad focuses on his job during the day and the television at night.
- Try to avoid displaying sexist attitudes and behaviors even in front of infants. You are a man and have many positive masculine traits to be proud of. Both your sons and daughters need to learn from them. Don't show your children the negative side of masculinity. They'll see enough of that as they grow older and begin to learn from people and things outside the nursery. Remember especially to avoid physical or verbal aggression and violence. You may not be Bill Cosby, but you don't have to act like Archie Bunker.
- Work hard to overcome the masculine part of your brain that inhibits your ability to be openly affectionate. This may be especially difficult for some men, but having a baby boy or girl around the house will soften you. Let it happen. Let it carry over to the way you treat your wife, your friends, your fellow workers.

- If you have an infant girl, you will probably find your-self treating her differently than you would a little boy. She will probably love staring into your eyes and smiling at you, which will make it easier for you to develop a close, intimate relationship with her. She will show you that she appreciates a gentle touch and a soothing sound, and that is how you will begin to treat her. But she isn't a piece of porcelain. In fact, most baby girls tend to be stronger and healthier than boys of the same age and can enjoy the physical stimulation you provide as much as boys would. She will let you know when you are being too rough and will be happiest when your behavior matches her basic temperament, interests, and abilities.

- Don't burden your infant daughter with sexist attitudes about the weaker sex. Encourage her to explore and conquer her physical environment jut as you would encourage a boy. Help her develop physical competence and reward her initiative and assertiveness. Help her exercise her physical abilities. Help her crawl up stairs. Roll a ball back and forth with her. Show her new places and things. Don't be afraid to take her to sporting events or expose her to physical activities appropriate for her age. Concentrate on these and other activities that will help her discover and develop her visual-spatial abilities. Tennis star Chris Evert credits the close, involved coaching of her father for much of her success in an obviously visual-spatial game.

- If you have an infant boy, you may find it difficult to form a sense of emotional intimacy with him. He would probably rather watch you wave a toy airplane around the room than stare into your eyes or babble at you. But keep reminding yourself that you also want to develop a close emotional relationship with him and that you want to help him learn to be appropriately expressive. Talk baby talk to him and help him exercise his verbal and interpersonal abilities the way you would exercise a girl's visual-spatial abilities. Read to him. Sing to him. Listen to music with him. Smile at him often and try to make a lot of eye contact. You won't change the sex of your children, but by following these suggestions with your boys and girls, you can help develop and strengthen all of their abilities. The brain, like a muscle, grows with exercise.

- Be aware of inborn tendencies in your baby. Some are more temperamental than others. Some are overly sensitive to loud noises or bright lights. Some like more physical activity than others. Be aware of the special qualities and abilities of your infant and encourage them. Be aware of the biological and social or environmental factors that may put your child at a disadvantage and work to overcome them. If you have an only child, for example, try to find opportunities for your baby to play with other children.

- Be especially alert to your infant's needs and moods. Your wife may be better at this than you are, but you can learn from her. Her brain and training have probably prepared her to be more sensitive to certain infant needs. Ask her how she always seems to know when the baby needs to be changed or fed, played with or put to sleep. Pay attention, and learn to be the best father you can be. Women bring their femaleness, men, their maleness, to parenting. Don't let your baby miss out on your half.

- Different levels and combinations of male and female hormones during pregnancy produce an infant brain that is more or less feminine, more or less masculine. But remember that the environment you, your wife, and society provide interacts with your baby's basic brain patterns to produce an endless variety of boys and girls who grow up to be wildly diverse.

LOOKING AHEAD

Joe's dad still sits him down to watch a basketball game once in a while, and Joe still pays about as much attention as he did two years ago when he was born. He might never learn to love basketball, but he has learned to love and rely on his father. He runs to the door when he hears Dad coming. He winds himself around Dad's leg when he wants to get bounced across the room. He watches Dad shave and makes it clear that he wishes he could do something so fascinating. In these and in hundreds of ways he shows how really attached he is to his father.

And his father is completely devoted to him. He has followed many of the suggestions offered in this chapter and feels totally bonded to his son. He knows how to take care of Joe and feels comfortable doing it. He didn't think he would have much in common with an infant, but he found out that he can really relate to his baby. He can read his son's expressions, understand his cries and his moods. He is constantly thinking about how Joe will react to different things, about how he will introduce Joe to new people and situations. He is fully aware of Joe's rapidly increasing abilities and his natural inclination toward mastery, competence, and self-assertion. And because of his special closeness to his son and his more adventurous attitude toward him, he is able to encourage those tendencies, often in ways that his wife does not. He knows how and when to encourage Joe to try a little harder and when to let him curl up in Mom's arms.

Joe's dad is also learning that being close to a baby can soften a man's heart. By spending so much time with an infant, he has learned that he can be more considerate and patient than he ever thought he could be—not only with Joe but with his wife and other people. He is learning from Joe just how capable he really is of intimacy and that he can be the kind of empathic person that so many men have trouble being. He has become the hugging and kissing kind of dad that he wasn't sure he could be. In the following chapters you will see how your positive involvement as a father increases the likelihood that not only you but your sons and daughters as well will develop a strong capacity for empathy. Later, you will discover that you have even given them the ability to become sensitive, caring parents themselves.

Joe loves all the attention he is getting. Consistent contact with two loving parents keeps him happy and comfortable but also exposes him to an ever-widening range of exciting experiences that will help prepare him to meet the challenges of his increasingly complex life.

REFERENCES

1. Greenberg, M., and Morris, N., "Engrossment: The Newborn's Impact Upon the Father." *American Journal of Orthopsychiatry*, Vol. 44, 1974, p. 520.

2. Parke, R., *Fathers*. Cambridge, MA: Harvard University Press.

3. Biller, H., and Salter, M., "Fathers, Mothers, and Infants Growing Together" *Lamaze Parents Magazine*, 1985.

4. Trotter, R., The Play's the Thing, *Psychology Today*, January 1987, p. 27.

5. Hall, H., "Carry On: A Cure for Chronic Crying." *Psychology Today*, Jan. 1987, p. 10.

6. Roberts, M., No Language But a Cry, *Psychology Today*, June 1987, p. 57.

7. Trotter, R., You've Come a Long Way Baby, *Psychology Today*, May 1987, p. 35.

8. Moir, A., and Jessel, D., *Brain Sex*. New York: Laurel, 1989.

9. Money, J., and Ehrhardt, A., *Man and Woman Boy and Girl*. Baltimore, MD: Johns Hopkins University Press, 1972.

10. Acherbach, J., "Why Are Men Better Than Women at Reading Maps?" Washington Post, October 16, 1992, p. D5.

11. Hopson, J., Marian Diamond: A Love Affair with the Brain, *Psychology Today*, November 1984, p. 62.

12. Kohlberg, L., and Zigler, E., "The Impact of Cognitive Maturity on the Development of Sex-role Attitudes in the Years Four–Eight" *Genetic Psychology Monographs*, Vol. 75, 1967, p. 89.

SUGGESTED READINGS

TOUCH POINTS: YOUR CHILD'S EMOTIONAL AND BEHAVIORAL DEVELOPMENT by Brazelton, T., Addison-Wesley, 1992.

WORKING PARENTS' SURVIVAL GUIDE by Olds, S., Prima Publishing, 1989.

SEPARATE LIVES: WHY SIBLINGS ARE SO DIFFERENT by Dunn, J., and Plomin, R., New York, Basic Books, 1990.

From Cradle to Kindergarten

STAGES OF INFANT DEVELOPMENT

With the accuracy of one of his country's famous time-pieces, noted Swiss psychologist Jean Piaget recorded thousands of observations of the most minute details of his children's behavior and from them crafted a whole new way of understanding the minds of babies. Piaget's carefully recorded observations paint a detailed picture of the developing mental abilities of babies and make it quite clear that infancy is not just a time for eating, sleeping, and crying. It is a period during which the awareness of objects and of cause and effect begins, all of the things that make up your baby's first step on the road to logical thinking.

You may not be as astute an observer as Piaget was, but if you have been watching closely, you will have seen your baby's mind awaken and go through the stages described by Piaget and observed in infants around the world. Babies differ, of course, with some seeming to be on daylight savings time and others being in another time zone altogether. The brains of infants born a month or two prematurely, for example, will be a month or two behind where Piaget or the calendar says they should be. Robust and exceptionally active babies who reach out to grab the world with gusto may develop a bit more quickly than their more timid brothers and sisters. But in general, most healthy babies do go through the mental stages described by Piaget on about the timetable his theory predicts.

A quick look at Piaget's work, his observations and experiments, will give you a good idea of what is happening as your baby progresses through the predicted stages. You will be able to see mental links being made and be amazed at how your baby's awareness of the world is growing. Even if you don't go to the lengths Piaget did, your constant awareness of your baby's emerging abilities will naturally strengthen the bond that is growing between you and your infant. Most of all, you will have fun watching your baby's abilities grow.

Piaget called infancy the sensory-motor period (from birth to about the second year) because during this time the first noticeable signs of intelligence in infants seem to be related to their senses and their motor activities, or physical movements. The first of the six stages of the sensory-motor period is characterized by the reflexive movements and relatively unorganized bodily reactions seen during the baby's first month of life. These reflexive movements are the basis for the more organized movements that gradually develop throughout the sensory-motor period. As a newborn, Piaget's daughter, Jacqueline, moved her hands reflexively until she accidentally made contact with a watch he held within her reach. Eventually she learned to follow the watch with her eyes and to reach it accurately.

> Laurent [at 9 days of age] is lying in bed and seeks to suck, moving his head to the left and to the right. Several times he rubs his lips with his hand which he immediately sucks. He knocks against a quilt and wool coverlet and each time he sucks the object, only to relinquish it after a moment and begins to cry. When he sucks his hand he does not turn away from it as he seems to do with the woolens, but the hand itself escapes him through lack of coordination. He then immediately begins to hunt again.[1]

Laurent's reflexive sucking of anything that came near his mouth gradually became specific sucking, with a definite preference for his thumb. He didn't know to avoid the nasty-tasting wool blanket at first, but he learned quickly. Your baby will probably learn just as quickly. Watch what happens as your baby reflexively sucks on and either accepts or rejects different objects.

During stage 2 (from one to four months), infants continue to broaden their range of behaviors by building on their reflexive actions. They make simple movements and repeat them over and over, apparently for the pure pleasure of doing them. Watch closely and you will see, for example, how your baby gradually becomes aware of his or her hands, the way Piaget did.

> Jacqueline seems not to have looked at her hands before (two months and 30 days). But on this date and the following she frequently notices her moving fingers and looks at

them attentively. At three months and 13 days when her hands move into her visual field she looks fixedly at them.[1]

During stage 3 (from four to eight months), infants begin to learn that some of the things they do make other things happen. And if something fun accidentally happens, they try to make it happen again, like the baby in Chapter 4 who learned to make the mobile move.

> Lucienne is lying in her bassinet. I hang a doll over her feet . . . her feet reach the doll right away and give it a violent movement which Lucienne surveys with delight. Afterward she looks at her motionless foot for a second, then recommences. There is no visual control over the foot, for the movements are the same when Lucienne only looks at the doll or when I place the doll over her head. On the other hand, the tactile control of the foot is apparent: after the first shakes, Lucienne makes slow foot movements as though to grasp and explore. For instance, when she tries to kick the doll and misses her aim, she begins again very slowly until she succeeds (without seeing her feet). In the same way I cover Lucienne's face or distract her attention for a moment in another direction; she nevertheless continues to hit the doll and control its movements.[1]

Lucienne was making something happen, but she didn't quite seem to understand how or why.

During the next stage (from eight to twelve months), infants appear to be trying to understand what effects their actions will have and begin to coordinate their behaviors in order to make things happen. They learn to reach for toys and things they want. However, if you move the toy out of sight, they will act as if it no longer exists. Babies are egocentric little things and are only aware of what exists in their own immediate experience. Gradually, after repeated experiences with things that swing, drop, or roll out of sight, they begin to realize that those things still exist and will look for them. Piaget says this, the concept of object permanence, is one of the most important achievements of the sensory–motor period.

Stage five (from 12 to 18 months) is characterized by directed groping. At this stage infants begin true experimentation. Instead of simply trying to reproduce behaviors discovered by accident, they try new ways of achieving ends. Their movements are directed. Piaget describes his son dropping one piece of bread at a time off the table and watching with great interest to see where each lands. According to Piaget, this was not just repeated behavior, as in earlier stages, but a serious attempt to find out what happens to dropped bread. Through such experiments infants gradually learn how to behave in order to achieve a desired goal.

Stage 6 (from eighteen months to about two years of age) marks the end of infantile, trial-and-error behavior and the beginning of true, logical thinking. By this time, children are able to see things in their mind and manipulate them mentally and then physically in order to achieve a goal. When Piaget offered his two-year-old son an upside-down bottle, the boy no longer tried to suck the wrong end. "He immediately displaces the wrong end with a quick stroke of the hand while looking beforehand in the direction of the nipple." He is showing the first signs of understanding the idea of physical space, which includes such things as the relationship of objects to each other, direction, distance, perspective and movement. Understanding these concepts is obviously important as your baby gradually learns to walk, get food from the plate to the mouth, and do anything that requires physical movement.

By having some idea how the infant body and mind operate, you will be better able to work with it as it goes through enormous changes—from an almost purely reflexive eating-sleeping machine to a walking-talking-thinking machine. Whether it be by playing with your watch, a doll, or an upside-down bottle, babies learn by meeting and exploring new people, places, and things, and the more meeting and exploring they do, the more competent and self-assured they will be as they grow older. You can't teach your infant to read or do algebra, but you can give babies a head start in two particular ways. When you are consistently involved and attentive, along with the baby's mother, you give infants a second source of physical, social, and intellectual stimulation, a second person to learn from, a second style of thinking and problem solving to imitate. And because moms and dads tend to treat babies differently, babies with involved dads get more than twice as much stimulation. They get different kinds of attention and stimulation.

A variety of tests are used to measure the physical, social, and intellectual competence of even very young babies. Researchers using these tests report that infants who have two closely involved parents tend to be more curious and eager to explore than those who do not have a close relationship with their fathers. Infants with involved fathers also seem to relate more maturely to strangers, react more competently in new situations, and be somewhat advanced in crawling, climbing, and manipulating things like spoons and toys.[2]

Tests of infants reared in families where, for one reason or another, the father was the primary caretaker, emphasize the special impact fathers can have on the mental and social development of their children. Infants in such families were tested shortly after birth and again two years later and found to be thriving and developing at a rapid rate. They scored higher, as if several months older, than the average on a wide range of skills and had especially impressive problem-solving abilities and social skills. They also showed high levels of curiosity and persistence—all traits that will be invaluable to them once they start school. Because the mothers in these families were regularly involved with their infants after work and on the weekends, it seems clear that the children benefited from having two committed parents rather than living in a more typical family in which the father's involvement with his infant is relatively limited.[3]

Being the primary caretaker and taking over a large share of responsibility is an excellent way for fathers to develop a close bond with their infants, but caretaking does not appear to be the most important factor in their stimulation. It is the overall level of involvement along with the degree of sensitivity to their needs that makes the difference to the infant.[4] The most competent infants seem to be those whose fathers help care for them but who also show high levels of affection and talk to and play actively with them.

Whether you are the primary caretaker during the day or just do your share in the morning and evening is not the issue. Your consistent daily involvement, for an hour or for several hours, is what makes a difference. Fathers who regularly get involved in relieving full-time mothers for an hour or two in the evening contribute greatly to their child's development as well as strengthen their marriages.[5]

- Remember that infants are not passive creatures just waiting to be fed or have their diapers changed. They are active and striving, gradually increasing their competence. They have a built-in need to explore and influence their world, and you should encourage their instinctive strivings by being closely involved with them.

- Give your baby a lot of visual stimulation. Hang all sorts of objects that can be touched and moved in front of your baby. You don't need to buy anything fancy or expensive. Your baby will be fascinated by jar tops, rag dolls, photographs, and almost anything you can think of. Encourage your baby to pay attention to new things. Point to pictures, name different objects, introduce a wide variety of toys when you play with your baby. The more you encourage infants to look at and play with new objects, the higher they are likely to score on intelligence tests.

- Watch your baby's eyes as you show them interesting things. Move things around in front of them and watch what happens. Help your baby learn to grasp and move things. Hide toys and see when your baby learns that they still exist, even if unseen. You could also buy a book on Piaget and use his theories and observations as a guide to help understand your baby's progress. You might even enjoy charting your baby's accomplishments. Most fathers will gladly tell you about their infant's latest milestone. But remember, it is your active involvement that counts, not whether you record all the details of your baby's development.

- Don't be overly concerned if your baby is not on the exact timetable Piaget predicts. Though many of the physical and intellectual stages in Piaget's theory do occur on a relatively predictable timetable, many do not. For example, most infants can lift their chins while lying on their stomachs at one month, sit and grasp objects at five or six months, stand by holding onto furniture at nine or ten months, and walk short distances by themselves at fourteen or fifteen months. Yet these stages are not set in stone, and babies differ in their rate of development with the different levels of encouragement and opportunities to practice they receive. Don't feel that you are a bad parent because a child in another family walks or talks at an earlier age than does your child.

- Learn more about your baby's emerging abilities and stimulate them by playing games like pat-a-cake and peek-a-boo that introduce them to the rules of social behavior. Even when infants are too young to play an active role, the structure of these repetitive games can help them grasp the turn-taking nature of social interactions.[6]

- Play tell me a story, in which you ask your infant to tell you a story. When the baby coos or makes other noises, you supply the words for the story. This helps teach babies that their responses will get responses from you.

- Play I'm gonna get you, in which you loom toward your baby saying things like "Ah, boom!" or "I'm gonna get you." This repetitious behavior should make your baby smile or laugh. Keep up the game until the baby stops responding.

- Play walking fingers or creepy crawlies, in which you use your fingers to crawl spiderlike up your baby's body. Babies love sensitive physical contact and will find your fingers fascinating.

- Play so big by extending your baby's arms and saying "So big!" Think up other simple games that give your baby a lot of visual, auditory, and tactile stimulation. One of the reasons infants find their fathers so exciting is that men tend to be more spontaneous and adventurous than women in the ways they play with babies and do things that many women wouldn't dream of doing.

- Watch your infant's reactions when you stop a game before the baby is ready to quit. You'll be amazed at the sophisticated levels of learning and communication you see. Canadian researchers found just that when they tested nineteen nine-month-old infants. They videotaped the infants as adults played several games with them. They stacked blocks and took turns toppling them, made squeaking noises with a toy, played peek-a-boo, and several other turn-taking games. However, after every four rounds of the game, the adult would stop and sit quietly for about fifteen seconds. The researchers analyzed the infants' actions and reactions and found that after only half an hour of play, the babies had begun to understand the games. During the interruptions, the babies made sounds and gestures that appeared to be asking the adults to take their turn. Many of them made signals that included the adult and the toy, such as showing the toy to the adult or alternating their gaze between the toy and the adult.[7]

- Don't confine your child often or for long periods of time. Life in a crib or playpen can be very boring for a child who is wide awake and ready for new things to do. When you have to use a playpen, try to position it so the baby does not feel isolated. In Russia, playpens are kept high off the floor at first, then lowered as the baby begins to stand. Your baby will learn much more from watching your hands and face than watching your feet.

- Give your baby as much freedom and confidence to explore the world as possible. Your attitude will influence your infant's explorations and development. Unless there is a safety or health hazard, think twice before restricting your baby. Pulling a few books off a shelf might offend your sense of order, but it will help your child discover new and exciting things about the world. On the other hand, infants do need constant supervision as they explore. They have a sense of self-preservation and aren't likely to crawl off the couch or bang into a door, but they are clumsy and accidents do happen.

- Give your child the maximum opportunity to explore and investigate by making your home as safe and accessible as possible. Remove fragile and dangerous items from low shelves and cabinets and replace them with old magazines, pots and pans, plastic dishes, and other suitable playthings. Don't worry about the mess. A cluttered (but safe) home is a sign of a healthy and curious baby.

- Don't use physical punishment when your baby begins to explore the world and accidentally breaks something. Even mild physical punishment, such as a light slap on the hand, will not teach the baby restraint and may discourage a child's natural curiosity. Researchers watched the way parents restrained their children and found that babies who were physically punished were no less likely than others to go on reaching for things again and again. And more importantly, children who were not punished scored higher than the others on tests of spatial skills and problem solving (fitting puzzle pieces together and putting pegs in a board), perhaps because they had been allowed more freedom to practice with and explore various parts of their world. [7]

- Keep a close watch on your infant's emerging abilities and change the environment when necessary so that your child is always learning from new things. If you stay aware of your infant's abilities, you will be able to create a learning environment that is appropriate yet challenging to your child's level of development. [8]

- Maintain a good relationship with your baby's pediatrician. You and your wife should both be involved in monitoring your baby's health and growth. Visit the pediatrician as a family and make sure you discuss any concerns you might have. The doctor is also a good source of information about appropriate development, particular milestones, and books you might want to consult to further your knowledge.

THE WILD CHILD

In the winter of 1799, a naked boy was seen running through the forests of southern France. Hunters captured this "wild child" on several occasions and exhibited him like an animal in a cage, but he was usually crafty enough to escape. After several captures and escapes, the French authorities finally brought the boy to Paris where he could be examined and studied by scientists. He is believed to have been about eleven years old at the time, and he had apparently lived alone in the wild for six or more years. Experts, including Phillipe Pinel, the father of psychiatry, examined the boy and concluded that he was an incurable idiot.

Jean Itard, a young French physician, thought differently, that the wild behavior of the child was the result of being isolated from human contact for a long time. Itard named the boy Victor and spent five years trying to educate him.

When Victor was captured, he walked and ran more like an animal than a human. When alone, he sat and rocked back and forth. When allowed out, he roamed around in freezing weather without clothes. He could grab food out of a pot of boiling water or out of a hot fire without showing signs of pain. He had a highly developed sense of smell but was unable to focus his eyes on anything for more than a few seconds. Victor could hear well but only sounds associated with food. He would turn toward the sound of a nut cracking but pay no attention to the sound of human voices. He made no attempts to communicate and seemed to see other humans as little more than obstacles to his wants and needs.

After more than five years with Itard, Victor had changed very little. He did learn to live in a house, sleep in a bed, wear clothes, and eat with a knife and fork. He even learned to focus his eyes, but he never learned to communicate very well. Itard managed to teach him to read, write, and understand a few simple words but no more. And Victor's social development was almost nonexistent. He seemed to have some affection for Itard and for the woman who cared for him, but he never learned to socialize with other people. He lived out a simple life and died at about the age of forty.

Victor was one of nature's experiments. Scientists couldn't send a baby into the woods to live alone just to see what would happen, but Victor's life makes it quite clear: Even though nature gives us a blueprint for development, it does not provide us with all that we need for what is considered normal human development. We need human contact. Denied this contact, Victor was physically, socially, and emotionally stunted. The results of millions of years of biological evolution are built into every newborn infant, but the results of millions of years of cultural evolution have to be acquired through social contact. And you, as the doting dad, will be one of the first and most important transmitters of culture to your children.

It began in infancy as you exhausted yourself getting up in the middle of the night, changing diapers and cleaning up messes. But now your baby is less dependent, and you are both in for some real fun as you go through the terrible twos. But don't worry. You won't have a wild child. These years aren't really going to be as terrible as you might have been led to expect. Two-year-olds are beginning to realize that there is life outside the playpen, that they have minds of their own and want to use them—but not always in ways you think they should. If you understand what their little minds and bodies are going through, you will be less likely to be frustrated by their attempts to test their developing physical and mental abilities.

- Don't expect your baby to grow up overnight. Even a precocious two- or three-year-old will still act like a baby from time to time. They'll whine or suck their thumbs or do something else that you think they should have grown out of. Don't become upset or frustrated with such babylike behaviors. A negative attitude is likely to make your child draw away from you and regress even more. Look at your own shortcomings and try to be more tolerant of those you see in your children.

- If you've had a bad day on the job or at the office, give yourself a chance to calm down and relax before dealing with your rambunctious toddler. This will minimize the likelihood of destructive power struggles. You aren't always at your best and neither are your children. You are more likely to be a kind and responsive father if you've had a good day than if you've had a bad day or are in a rotten mood. Similarly, tired, hungry, or frustrated toddlers will act more like babies than when they are well rested, have just eaten, and are receiving your loving attention.

- When you do feel tense or upset, try to explain your feelings to your children, "I'm frustrated . . . I had a hard day," "I'm not angry at you. The car had a flat tire." It is important to let children know that you can get upset or angry for reasons that have nothing to do with them.

- Learn to negotiate with your increasingly verbal and sometimes defiant child. Remember that babies stop being babies and begin asserting their independence more between eighteen and twenty-four months of age. This transition is not always easy for children or parents. Your baby will become less and less dependent on you and try to take more and more control of things. "I'll do it myself!" is a typical two-year-old's cry. If they don't get to do it, they may become quite stubborn and negative. This is a preview of the kind of rebelliousness you are likely to see in adolescence, but toddlerhood has its own special qualities, which you should make the most of.

- Don't be upset because you are losing control of your once totally dependent little bundle of joy. Rather, look forward to encouraging your toddler's emerging self-reliance. Work hard to balance your child's need for independence with your need to be an encouraging supervisor. It's your responsibility to learn how to keep calm and to relax. If you don't let yourself get too frustrated, you'll burst with pride at your toddler's daily accomplishments.

- Be prepared to hear some interesting, unpredictable, and disconcerting things from the mouths of babes. "I don't want her. You can have her. She's too fat for me," one three-year-old sang to his brother in front of their overweight mother. Try not to feel hurt or threatened by such things. Try to laugh them off and remember that children have to exercise their rapidly expanding vocabulary.

- Watch your own mouth. Children are great imitators, and they like to repeat what they hear. Avoid foul language if you don't want your children repeating it. Don't be overly sarcastic in front of the kids. They may mimic your words without really understanding their significance. But no matter how calm and well spoken you are, toddlers are likely, at least occasionally, to let you know that they don't like your demands or behavior. You may not like hearing these things, but it is important for your children's emotional and intellectual development for you to allow them to express themselves. Don't let them be verbally destructive, but do allow them to express their thoughts and feelings freely.

UNDERSTANDING DEVELOPMENTAL ADVANCES

Piaget's ground-breaking studies and fascinating observations of his children, which began in the 1920s, encouraged several generations of psychologists to follow in his footsteps. Over the years, they have developed hundreds of tests and different ways of broadening our understanding of the child's mind. Psychologist John H. Flavell and his colleagues at Stanford University, for example, are studying children's grasp of the distinction between appearance and reality. One of the things they use is a joke-store sponge that looks life a piece of granite. When you pick it up, you immediately realize that it is a sponge. "A 3-year-old probably wouldn't be so sure," says Flavell. "Children at this age often aren't quite able to grasp the idea that what you see is not always what you get. By the time they are 6 or 7 years old, however, most children have a fair grasp of the appearance/reality distinction that assumes so many forms in our daily lives. Misperceptions, misexpectations, misunderstandings, false beliefs, deception, play and fantasy . . . ".[9]

For the past ten years, Flavell and his colleagues have been asking questions about sponge rocks and using other ways of finding out what children of different ages know about the difference between appearance and reality. First, they give children a brief lesson on the difference between appearance and reality by showing them, for instance, a Charlie Brown puppet inside a ghost costume. Then they explain that Charlie Brown "looks like a ghost to your eyes right now" but is "really and truly Charlie Brown" and that "sometimes things look like one thing to your eyes when they are really and truly something else."

Next, the researchers show the children a number of illusory objects, like the sponge rock, and ask them questions about the reality and appearance of the objects: "What is this really and truly; is it really and truly a sponge or is it really and truly a rock?" "When you look at this with your eyes right now, does it look like a rock or does it look like a sponge?"

In another test, they show a three-year-old and a six-year-old a red toy car covered by a green filter that makes it look black. They give the children the car to inspect, then put it behind the filter again and ask: "What color is this car? Is it red or is it black?" The three-year-old is likely to say "black"; the six-year-old, "red." Similar procedures are used to investigate children's awareness of the distinction between real and apparent size, shape, events, and the presence or absence of a hidden object.

"In all these tests," Flavell explains, "most three-year-old children have difficulty making the distinction between appearance and reality. They often err by giving the same answer (appearance or reality) to both questions. However, they rarely answer both questions incorrectly, suggesting that the mistakes are not random; the children are simply having conceptual problems with the distinction. By the time they are 6 or 7, however, most children get almost all the questions right."

Flavell and hundreds of researchers around the world have been fine-tuning and filling in Piaget's original theory, adding a bit here, subtracting a bit there. The predicted mental advances don't happen on as strict a schedule as Piaget set forth. Instead, they occur gradually over months and years, depending on a child's biology and experience. The wild child didn't have much experience with human faces and never learned to recognize them very well. He had little experience with language and never learned to speak very well. On the other hand, his life alone in the forest gave him a number of remarkable physical abilities.

Piaget's theories continue to be refined, but in general, researchers are finding that the stages of mental development he described are relatively similar from child to child in every culture. And brain researchers are finding the same thing. Piaget, for example, traced mental development through four major age-related stages: from birth to two years of age, from two to seven, from seven to eleven, and from twelve through adulthood. Behavioral studies, like those of Flavell, suggest that children do make major intellectual gains at about the ages of two, seven, and twelve. Now, there is evidence that the brain goes through a series of growth spurts that correlate quite well with Piaget's stages. When electroencephalographic measures were made of 577 children ranging in age from two months to young adulthood, five major growth spurts, or increases in the rate of brain growth, were found that could account for the mental and behavioral changes observed by Piaget. They occur from birth to about three years of age, from four to six, from eight to ten, from eleven to fourteen, and from fifteen to adulthood. These findings strongly favor the idea that there is a genetically programmed unfolding of specific brain connections at relatively specific ages.[10]

If you are an involved father, you are probably quite aware of how your infant negotiated the stages of the so-called sensory-motor period. In the remarkable first two years of life, you saw a tremendous growth in your baby's ability to understand and change the physical and social worlds. But two-year-olds still have a long way to go. They are entering what Piaget calls the preoperational period (from about two years to seven years). This is the time when children begin to develop the ability to perform internal mental operations, as opposed to purely physical operations. During the sensory-motor stage, for example, children learn to reach for a toy they see and want. In the preoperational stage, they learn to think about and ask for toys even when the toys are out of sight. With this ability to imagine the world, children begin to play at make-believe. By pretending to be someone else (a parent, teacher, or doctor), they begin to learn the customs and manners of people around them.

You won't be able to see inside your child's head, but some of Piaget's experiments vividly demonstrate the mental changes that are taking place. Take two balls of soft clay of equal size and show them to your child. Once the child agrees that the balls are the same size, roll one of them out into a long sausage shape and ask if the two pieces are still equal, if they still contain the same amount of clay. A child in the preoperational stage will usually say that the sausage shape contains more clay because it is longer. Roll the sausage back into a ball, and they will again agree that both balls contain the same amount of clay. By the time your child is six or seven (sometimes called the age of reason), these changes won't seem so hard to understand. If you make the sausage very long and thin, your child may still say that it is bigger than the ball. But if the sausage is short and fat, the child will probably realize that it contains the same amount of clay as the ball.

With these emerging mental abilities, terrible two-year-olds gradually turn into amazing three-, four-, and five-year-olds. By three or three and a half years of age, most children begin to settle down. They become much less self-centered and much easier to deal with. They are likely to be more calm and to have fewer unsettling mood swings. Some may still seem impulsive and moody at times but less often than a year earlier. If you have had a tough time dealing with your two-year-old, be patient. Things get better. As they grow older, children develop a greater ability to wait and to pay attention. They begin to use their imaginations to think and plan ahead, at least with respect to the next hour or so. Your child may now be asking to do something tonight or tomorrow rather than demanding that it be done immediately.

Many, if not most, boys and girls seem to have both relatively settled and unsettled periods during different phases of childhood. For most children, somewhere between four and a half and five and a half, there is another settling-down period. Temper tantrums may still occur, but many extremely rambunctious four-year-olds seem to quiet down and become more mature, realistic, and cooperative by their fifth birthdays. A mature four- or five-year-old will begin to understand right from wrong with regard to other people's feelings and property. Five-year-olds are less likely than younger children to be bullies, to tease, or to take the toys of others. They begin to understand the consequences of their behavior and have some awareness of their growing maturity. You are likely to hear your five-year-old say "Dad, remember when I couldn't even hop on one foot?" "Wasn't it funny how I didn't know which was my right hand when I was a little kid." A five-year-old may even talk in a very realistic way about what he or she will do as a teenager or adult. A four-year-old's fantasies are often quite outlandish, but a five-year-old's may be surprisingly mature.

By the time they are six or seven, most children are entering what Piaget calls the stage of concrete operations, and their thinking begins to speed up. If you try the ball of clay trick with them now, they will take one look and realize that it contains the same amount of clay no matter what shape you roll it into. During the stage of concrete operations, children learn to think about concrete or solid objects without having to experiment with them. A few years earlier, your child might have searched every room in the house for a lost toy. Now, the little thinker can sit back and try to remember where the toy might be. As their thinking continues to speed up and become more concrete, they become much more goal oriented and better able to realize the steps involved in an activity and the need to plan ahead. They usually have a better attention span and are able to concentrate on what they are doing. And these are among the abilities they will need as they get ready to march off to school.

To help your children as their development advances, you should do the following.

- Be aware of age/stage developmental milestones and help your child master them. But don't worry if your child is a week or a month or even more behind schedule. There are striking differences among children at all ages, and there are many reasons why a toddler might be ahead or behind the schedule described by Piaget and other psychologists. Children who have been sick a lot during infancy may be behind because they didn't get as much time as other children to run around and play and discover the world. Children who have not had a lot of social contact or who have not spent much time with other children may also lag in social development. If you stay closely involved in every stage of your child's development, you will be able to help in areas where help is needed. If you think there may be a problem in any area, don't hesitate to consult a specialist.

- Be patient. Your three- or three-and-a-half-year-old child may begin to question everything with a chronic *why?* But this isn't a return to the terrible twos. It is an increasingly sophisticated attempt to understand and begin to take control of the world. Don't get annoyed. Try to encourage and satisfy your child's curiosity and growing independence.
- Don't yell at your kids. Researchers have found that soft words speak louder with toddlers. They tested how well children listen to what they are told to do by giving a variety of positive (Clap your hands!) and negative (Don't touch your toes!) commands to three- to four-year-olds and five- to six-year-olds. The commands were given in either a soft, medium, or loud voice. When the orders were given in soft tone, the kids did what they were told. But when the adults yelled, something strange happened. The older children obeyed, but the younger ones did the opposite of what they were told. Why? Because children younger than five tend to obey the energy of instructions first and only then interpret the meaning. A loud "don't" gets their attention, then they only follow the second part of the command.[11] Make sure you speak softly

and explain exactly what you expect, especially with young children.

- Don't get your kicks through your children. Too many five-year-olds, and even younger children, get pushed into various types of highly structured lessons and organized activities their parents believe they may have enjoyed at that age. The kids may go along with such things in order to please you, but they may get no real sense of satisfaction out of it. Don't exploit your child's desire to please just so you can brag about his or her accomplishments. It's okay to enjoy those accomplishments, but remember that children have to enjoy them too. Let them develop their sense of self-determination.

- Give your children the opportunity to develop their talents and their sense of self-respect. Help them be proud of what they can do, not crushed by their limitations. Children don't have to be pushed or pressured into expressing their interests and abilities. Your support, acceptance, and patience will help them develop a strong sense of competence and confidence.

- Encourage your toddlers to be self-reliant in such things as washing themselves and playing alone. By age three most children are ready to learn such things, and they usually want to impress you with their growing competence. Applaud them and encourage them to become even more self-reliant.

- Don't get carried away with your toddler's abilities. There will be times when you think your child is a budding genius. But even if children have an excellent memory for details or can pronounce words well when reading out loud, it does not mean they can think like adults.

- If your son or daughter is precocious, remember that children also need to develop their social and emotional skills. Do not make the mistake of separating them from other children for special training. Gifted children should be encouraged to develop a wide range of interests, including those in which they may not be exceptional. Their intellectual gifts will not fade or stagnate as long as they have a reasonably stimulating environment. In fact, intellectually gifted children (as well as those who may be especially talented in other areas) will probably make much better use of their special talents if you encourage them to develop into well-rounded individuals rather than channeling all of their efforts into one pursuit.[12]

- Be prepared to hear some interesting things from toddlers. They have a remarkable spurt in language ability between the ages of two and four, and by age five they may be quite impressed with their verbal creations, believing them, for example, to be exceedingly humorous even when you find them incomprehensible or disgusting. Don't be surprised if your preschooler becomes obsessed with talking about genitalia or what goes on in the bathroom. At this stage, children are flexing their verbal powers and curiosity. It's best to give a quick response to this kind of talk and then move on to something else.

- Remember that boys and girls are different, and as they grow older, those differences become more apparent because of biology and because of increasing social pressures on them to be different. More boys like to do things that enhance their physical and spatial skills; girls, their verbal and personal skills. Boys explore the physical world more; girls, the personal world.[13]

- Encourage your boy or girl to grow in directions you think are appropriate, but remember that it is not your job to push him or her into some rigid stereotypical sexist—or extremely nonsexist—role. If your children have a clearly established sense of themselves, they will feel secure enough to broaden their range of skills and transcend narrow gender stereotypes as they mature. A boy who is secure in his masculinity will not be afraid of being called a sissy if he decides that he wants to take cooking lessons. A girl who is secure about her femininity won't be afraid to fight for a spot on the baseball team.

REFERENCES

1. Piaget, J., *Six Psychological Studies*. New York: Random House, 1967.

2. Biller, H., *Fathers and Families: Paternal Factors in Child Development*. Westport, CT: Auburn House, 1993; Biller, H. B. Wolman (Ed.) *Handbook of Developmental Psychology*, New York: Prentice Hall, 1982.

3. Pruett, K., *The Nurturing Father*. New York: Warner Books, 1987.

4. Easterbrooks, M., and Goldberg, W., "Toddler Development in the Family: Impact of Father Involvement and Parenting Characteristics" *Child Development*, Vol. 55, 1984, p. 740.

5. Biller, H., and Solomon, R., *Child Maltreatment and Paternal Deprivation, A Manifesto for Research, Prevention and Treatment*. Lexington, MA: Lexington Books, 1986.

6. Trotter, R., The Play's the Thing, *Psychology Today*, January 1987, p. 27.

7. Fischman, J., "Games Babies Play," *Psychology Today*, October 1987, p. 14.

8. Moss, R., "Use the Rod, Spoil the Child," *Psychology Today*, November 1986, p. 16.

9. Flavell, J., Really and Truly, *Psychology Today*, January 1986, p. 38.

10. Trotter, R., "Growth Spurts Mirror Mental Milestones, *Psychology Today*, September 1987, p. 13.

11. Kalter, J., Soft Words Speak Louder with Kids, *Psychology Today*, December 1983, p. 14.

12. Biller, H., and Meredith, D., *Father Power*, New York: David McKay, 1974.

13. Biller, H., in Lamb, M., (Ed.) *The Role of the Father in Child Development*, New York: Wiley, 1981; Ilg, F., Ames, L., and Baker, S., *Child Behavior*, New York: Harper & Row, 1981.

SUGGESTED READINGS

BETWEEN FATHER AND CHILD: HOW TO BECOME THE KIND OF FATHER YOU WANT TO BE by Levant, R. and Kelly, J., Penguin, 1989.

KNOW YOUR CHILD: AN AUTHORITATIVE GUIDE FOR TODAY'S PARENTS by Chess, S. and Thomas, A., Basic Books, 1989.

THE PRESCHOOL YEARS by Galinsky, E. and David, J., Times Books, 1988.

MISEDUCATION: PRESCHOOLERS AT RISK by Elkind, D., Knopf, 1987.

Self-Confidence, Morality, and Discipline

We all want good, happy children. And since you are reading this book, you probably agree that our children are our most precious commodity. We love them, we cherish them, and we want nothing but the best for them. Surprising as it may seem, however, childhood has not always been a rose garden. In fact, says Lloyd de Mause, author of *The History of Childhood*, childhood is "a nightmare from which we have only recently begun to awaken".[1] In his almost unbelievable book, de Mause documents eras in which it was common practice to kill, abandon, abuse, and terrorize even the youngest of children and goes on to describe what he sees as significant stages in the history of childhood. The first stage was characterized by infanticide, the murder of infants, a practice that appears to have been socially accepted from prehistoric times until about the fourth century A.D. The writings of early Greeks and Romans, for instance, contain hundreds of references to infanticide. Among wealthy families, the firstborn child was usually allowed to live if it was healthy. But other children, especially if they were girls or if they were illegitimate, were often killed. Roman law did not even consider the killing of children as murder until A.D. 347. Infanticide was so common that even the ancient historians blamed it for the depopulation of both Greece and Rome.

When infants were allowed to live, they were not always kept by their parents. Abandonment characterized the second stage of the history of childhood (from the fourth to the thirteenth century). Records from this period show that many children in western Europe were sold as slaves or servants, and many were given away or abandoned to monasteries and nunneries. Some were even mutilated and sold as beggars. A blind child or one with a crushed foot or amputated limb excited more pity and collected more alms.

The most common form of abandonment during the Middle Ages began with a wet nurse, a woman who suckles other women's children. Parents who could afford it sent their children to live in the home of a wet nurse for the first two to five years of life. After that children were usually cared for by servants and then sent off to school or to work. Parents spent a minimum of time rearing their children.

As depressing as this history may seem, there is a brighter side. The quality of child care has improved progressively throughout history. Gradually, parents began to pay more attention to their children although not always in the most positive of ways. In the seventeenth century, for example, John Locke described the child's mind as a "tabula rasa," or a clean slate on which parents and educators tried to write. Often, they tried very hard, too hard, to mold children. Strict discipline was thought to be necessary to learning, and de Mause says that a large percentage of children born prior to the eighteenth century were what today would be called battered children. Beatings began in infancy and were a regular part of a child's life. Whips of all kinds, shovels, canes, iron and wooden rods, and special instruments designed to raise blisters were used to discipline children at home and in school.

By the eighteenth century, a real change in the treatment of children was becoming apparent. In England, societies for the prevention of cruelty to children were created. Children were still beaten and punished, but they were no longer subjected to regular whippings. The ideas of Locke were replaced by those of Jean Jacques Rousseau, who described the infant as a "noble savage," unspoiled by the pressures of parents, teachers, and society. He said children should be allowed to grow and develop in an atmosphere of freedom and learn from their experiences and interactions with their world. Unlike Locke, Rousseau did not believe that education should be forced on children. Let them develop naturally, he urged, and at about the time of puberty their minds would be ready for formal education and training. The eighteenth century also saw the birth of pediatrics and a gradual but steady decline in the infant death rate.

In the nineteenth century, scientific interest in children blossomed with a boost from Charles Darwin, who published a day-to-day record of the development of his son. Near the end of the last century in the United States, psychologist G. Stanley Hall began to investigate the development of children, and his books on educating children were among the first to be used in colleges. Since Hall's time, thousands of books about child development have been written, and the history of childhood continues to change. Child abuse and child neglect are still serious problems, but de Mause calls the second half of the twentieth century the "helping stage" in the history of childhood. Parents, teachers, and government policy are actively focused on helping and nurturing children, and a number of groups, such as the Children's Defense Fund, advocate for the welfare of all children.

Unfortunately, *nurturing* has often been too narrowly equated with *mothering*. During the current stage in the history of childhood, the definition of *nurturing* will have to be expanded to include *fathering*. Only with the active involvement of committed mothers and fathers can we begin to produce well-rounded boys and girls, children who are themselves nurturing as well as self-confident, properly assertive, and morally mature.

Research consistently shows, for example, that the most well-adjusted adults are those who spent a good deal of time during childhood with loving fathers. In one study, college students who had taken a personality test filled out a detailed questionnaire about how much time their fathers had spent at home and how close they had been to them when they were children.[2] The most well-adjusted students were those who rated their fathers as at least moderate in both nurturance and availability. In other words, fathers who had consistent and relatively warm contact with their children helped provide a good foundation for their children's later adjustment. These students were likely to see themselves as dependable, trusting, practical, and friendly. Poorly adjusted students were more likely to describe themselves as aloof, anxious, inhibited, and unfriendly. The most poorly adjusted students came from families in which the father was rarely available and was cold and distant when he was home. This is not surprising, because an uncaring dad is obviously not a good role model for his children. It is also not surprising that students tended to have adjustment problems when their fathers were home a lot but were cold and distant. In such homes, children are likely to feel inadequate and insecure because their fathers do not appear to care about them or their activities.

What is surprising is that students who had loving and affectionate but frequently absent fathers were also likely to have adjustment problems. Repeated separations from a loving father are likely to frustrate a child, especially if the absences are inconsistent and unpredictable. Your child may begin to doubt your love.

Other studies have found that children with nurturing fathers are also more likely to be generous and altruistic. Psychologists Eldred Rutherford and Paul Mussen passed out bags of candy to four-year-old boys at a nursery school and told them to give some to two other children they liked best. Those who were the most generous with their candy tended to be those who described their fathers as warm, affectionate, and comforting.[3] Research also suggests that the effects of active fathering have a long-term impact on children's ability to be empathetic and caring toward others. As part of a twenty-five-year study, psychologist David McClelland and his colleagues looked at information gathered on kindergarten children and found that those who had affectionate fathers were much more likely to grow up to be tolerant and understanding adults than were those whose fathers had been relatively uninvolved with them. The investigators concluded that when both the father and mother are nurturing and accepting, it is much more likely that their child will develop into a socially and morally mature adult.[4] The same research suggests a connection between close, loving fathering during the preschool years and successful relationships during midlife. People who had warm and loving fathers were likely to have achieved long-term marriages, parenthood, and close friendships.[5]

How can you help your child develop into a confident, loving, well-adjusted adult?

- Be there for your children as much and as often as possible and learn to nurture, or truly father, them. If possible, try to spend two hours a day with your children at least through the preschool and the early elementary school years. If you are a loving and ever-present factor in their lives, you will be an effective limit setter as well as a role model for assertiveness, independence, and moral development in your sons and daughters.

- Express your love for your children openly. You may find it difficult at first, but the extra effort will be worth it, especially when you see the glow that a loving comment can put on a young child's face. It's never too late to start—hug your kid today. You might start something that you won't be able to stop. If you don't start now, you might never be able to. It's easy to hug your toddler, and if you make it a practice, you might be hugging a loving teenager in a few years. If you don't start when your children are young and cuddly, you may never overcome your fear of intimacy, never be able to hug your children as they grow older and less cuddly. Make sure you love what you have created.

- Be as loving as you can but remember that nurturing isn't just hugs and kisses and saying "Daddy loves you." You can make your children feel loved and secure just by being around the house and paying attention to what they are doing, by supporting their interests and applauding their achievements. When kids do something they are proud of, they want to know that you are proud of them too.

- Show your love, but don't completely hide your negative emotions. Let them know when you are upset, but avoid expressing your feelings in ways that may be harmful or abusive to your children. Don't ever lose control and call your child derogatory or hateful names or say you hate your child. On the other hand, don't be afraid to let your child know when something is bothering you. Don't just sit there and bite your lip the next time the car won't start. Express your frustrations and explain why you are upset. Your child will be impressed that an all-powerful daddy is capable of showing strong and appropriate emotions. Children are sensitive to emotional nuances and may misinterpret your mood changes if you don't explain them. Being egocentric, younger children are especially likely to think they caused your anger, sadness, or frustration.

- Don't worry that being too loving will undermine your authority. The more you express your feelings of affection, the more likely your children will respect your opinions and expectations. Your closeness to your wife and children will also make it easier for your wife to control the children. Psychologist Hugh Lytton found that mothers are much more successful and comfortable in setting limits for their children when fathers are a real part of the parenting team. Children with nurturing fathers are more likely to obey their mothers when the father is present and especially when he explicitly supports her requests.[6]

- Don't worry that being too loving will spoil your children or will make them overly dependent. The most competent children have fathers who are nurturing but also encourage independence. If you are overly stern in an attempt to produce self-reliance, you may get the opposite effect. Love and kindness, not strictness, is more likely to lead to independence and self-reliance because it gives a child the confidence upon which to build competence. It can also make family life a lot more peaceful. Encourage each accomplishment, whether it be tying a shoelace or writing a term paper. The more recognition you give children for their achievements, the less likely they will be to try to get your attention by throwing tantrums, screaming, or yelling.

- Don't be a sugar daddy or try to make up for your shortcomings as a father by showering your kids with gifts. This will not make up for your frequent absences or your inability to express your love in more meaningful ways.

- Don't use gifts to gain a feeling of control over your family. Gift getting is one of the greatest joys of childhood. Remember all those birthdays, Christmasses, Hanukkahs, and other gift-getting occasions and how excited—or disappointed—you were? You'll love surprising your kids with all kinds of things, but don't overdo it as many parents, especially fathers, do. Giving too much raises their expectations and increases the chances that they will be disappointed in the future. Remember that the most precious gift you can give a child is your consistent loving support, interest, and attention.

- Don't use gifts to satisfy your own needs. There is

nothing wrong with buying a child something you always wanted as a child, but remember that your child may not want what you wanted. An unwanted gift may backfire on you if your child feels pressured to use it.
- Don't be afraid to tell your children what you can and cannot afford. Let them know when it is not reasonable for you to buy what they want. Begin to teach them about some of the economic realities of life at an early age.

INDEPENDENCE AND AGGRESSIVENESS

Charlie, an energetic four-year-old, had only been in a full-time day-care program for six weeks when his parents were called in for a meeting. Charlie, they were told, was a terror with the other children. If someone bumped into him or if Charlie thought someone had made a face at him, he would immediately lash out. When Charlie's behavior was described by the teacher, his father responded with pride rather than dismay. He insisted that Charlie was just acting assertively and sticking up for his rights. He said he felt proud every time his son told him he had been in a fight at school. Charlie's mother smiled in agreement as her husband described their child-rearing philosophy.

Instead of trying to reason with these parents, the teacher decided to let them see what their philosophy had produced. They went to the window and watched Charlie on the playground. Charlie had never been mean or nasty at home, but his father saw him punch a boy for not throwing a ball to him, take a jump rope away from a little girl, and kick another child who was in his way. Charlie's parents saw that they had produced a bully.

Many otherwise loving and nurturing fathers make the same mistake Charlie's parents made. They encourage aggressiveness, especially in their sons, without teaching them self-control and respect for the rights of others. Assertiveness has a definite and important place in every child's life and should not be smothered in either boys or girls. But being assertive means more than being physically aggressive. It means making yourself heard, standing up for your rights, and having the confidence to do what you think is right. Children need to learn how to communicate their choices and preferences. They need the confidence to resist arbitrary control by parents, teachers, and the playground bully.

You, as a father, will play an especially important role in helping both your sons and daughters develop a useful sense of assertiveness and independence. You are likely to be more naturally aggressive than your wife and to be in more situations where self-assertion is expected. By being appropriately aggressive and sensitive in those situations, you are showing children how to be effectively assertive themselves. If you are punitive and insensitive, you are teaching them to be the same. And if you use physical punishment in response to your children's aggressive behavior, you may make them even more aggressive. They may come to see physical aggression as the best way to deal with other children. They may also be frustrated by your punitiveness and take it out on other children because they can't retaliate against you.

To help your kids find the right balance between assertiveness and respect for others, you should do the following:

- Don't let your babies grow up to be bullies. A twenty-two year study of 800 children found that children as young as six have already developed a specific behavior pattern—either aggressive or social—and that the aggressive boys and girls were still aggressive at age nineteen. By the time they were thirty, they were more likely to be social and educational failures, to have been in trouble with the law, and to have emotional problems.[7]

- Teach your children the difference between appropriate and destructive aggression. For example, let them get angry at you, but don't let them become verbally or physically abusive. As long as a child's expression of frustration or anger does not become abusive or destructive, it can be a healthy outlet.

- Don't be afraid to argue with your children in a constructive manner. Allow them to disagree with you. Don't just say "I'm the boss," and force them to follow your orders. Give them a chance to express their opinions and preferences. A healthy argument is a good way to teach young children how to assert themselves without resorting to tantrums or physical aggression to get their way. Use intelligent, patient arguments to show children that your decisions are based on reason rather than arbitrary power. It will teach them to deal similarly with others. There is a big difference between discussion with a two-year-old and a twelve-year-old. But when you are patient, even two-year-olds may be surprisingly cooperative. On the other hand, twelve-year-olds may still be throwing tantrums if you were not willing to consider their side of arguments when they were two. They will probably be totally uninterested in your opinions.

- If your child's behavior begins to get out of hand, provide a cooling-off period for both of you. Sometimes it is best to leave the room, making it clear that abusive behavior or language will not be rewarded with any further attention. Later, provide a calm atmosphere and let your child voice complaints and frustrations. Tensions can be lowered even if no immediate solution to the problem is found.

- Don't feel that your child's anger is a threat to you or a sign of ungratefulness. It is only a natural reaction to one of the many frustrations of childhood. As your children mature, their anger will become more appropriate, more directed at both their own failures and disappointment at the unreasonable behavior of others.

- Don't forbid a child to challenge the opinions of authority figures, including yourself. Extreme deference to adults is all too often considered the hallmark of the well-behaved child, but such expectations can encourage a child to become inhibited and passive instead of being constructively assertive.

- Remember that assertiveness goes hand in hand with self-confidence and independence. Encourage your child's attempts to reach higher and go farther. If you are forever worried about injuries and accidents, you may raise an overly dependent child who always turns to others for support and protection. Let your boys and girls tackle the high bar on the jungle gym. Just be there to catch them when they fall.

- Encourage independence, but don't push too hard. What counts is that your child is making gradual improvements. Children need your patience and encouragement, whether it is learning how to tie shoelaces, ride a bike, or do long division.

- Stay closely involved with your wife in fostering independence in your children. Some mothers tend to be overly protective, especially with their firstborn. They may be afraid of injury and likely to stifle their children's active play and exploration. On the other hand, many fathers tend to expect too much autonomy and independence, particularly from a son, and force their children into excessive self-reliance. When you and your wife are both closely involved with your children, your combined expectations can offset each other and result in a more realistic and less extreme approach.

- Don't put too much pressure on a relatively shy and timid child to be assertive. Instead, help a timid child gradually build self-confidence. Encourage children to be assertive in ways that are compatible with their personalities. Some children need help to control their natural aggressiveness. Others need help overcoming their natural inhibitions.

- Be an available and effective role model for your children and help them develop confidence and self-esteem by letting them take part in some of your chores, hobbies, or other activities. And when you do, be patient. Focus on your relationship with the child, not the task at hand. The joy of sharing a job will usually outweigh the additional time the job may take. Do a little planning ahead and make sure your child has the appropriate "tools" for the job. Don't expect your preschooler to be much help painting the house. Instead, use your imagination to find some child-sized jobs that will let your little helper feel proud of being part of the team.

- As your children grow older, encourage more and more responsibility. Let them help plan meals or prepare a family cookout. You'll probably be surprised at what your youngster can do given the chance. But even if a young child tires easily and loses interest, he or she still had that opportunity to be involved with you. Try to enjoy what you are doing together. If you don't like it, your child probably won't get much fun out of it either. Find jobs that both of you will enjoy. You may even find that some jobs you don't ordinarily like may be a lot more fun when you and your child do them together.

- Don't be sexist in your choice of activities for your sons and daughters. Be supportive of both sons and daughters who take an interest in your work. Girls need the confidence they can gain by doing things outside the traditional feminine world. However, remember that children do much better when given a choice about participating in your activities. Some children, no matter what sex, simply are not interested in painting the house or preparing a meal. Despite how flexible or liberated you may be, they may feel that certain jobs simply are not right for them. You can encourage your children to be more open-minded, but don't force the issue.

- Remember that your daughters will probably need extra help in learning how to assert themselves. Despite all efforts to redefine masculine and feminine roles, biology and society still conspire to make little boys assertive and independent while teaching little girls to avoid overly aggressive or competitive behavior. Don't shortchange your daughters by inhibiting their competitiveness. Don't force gender stereotypes on boys or girls. Try to give both the confidence to be dynamic and assertive in whatever they choose to do.

HELPING YOUR CHILDREN AVOID FEAR OF SUCCESS

After first-term finals, Anne finds herself at the top of her medical school class.

After first-term finals, John finds himself at the top of his medical school class.

Psychologist Matina Horner asked young college women to write a story about Anne and asked young men to write about John. The women tended to write stories emphasizing Anne's conflict between doing well in medical school and her anxiety over romantic relationships. A common story ending involved Anne deliberately reducing her level of performance, getting married, and dropping out of medical school. The men tended to emphasize John's dedication, striving, achievement orientation, and self-confidence.[8]

Horner's experiment was one of the first to highlight the clear-cut gender stereotypes that have discouraged many women from pursuing certain types of careers. It vividly demonstrated that many women actually seemed to fear that if they did well in traditionally masculine areas, they would be considered aggressive and unfeminine. They feared that the consequences of success might involve being rejected by friends, lovers, and family.

That was thirty years ago, and we've come a long way since then. But parents, especially fathers, still have a long way to go in encouraging equal assertiveness and achievement in their sons and daughters. And they should start when their children are toddlers, when they are making their first important achievements. Fathers are especially important in helping their daughters avoid fear of success, because it is little boys—and then men— who will be most likely to ridicule girls—and then women—who are smart and aggressive and don't want to be turned into Stepford wives. A loving, encouraging father can assure his daughter that even if some boys and men are threatened by competent women, he like many other men will respect her and find her admirable and attractive.

- Don't let unrealistic fears about how delicate your daughter is keep you from encouraging her competence in any area. Most fathers feel more protective toward daughters than sons, but don't let your attitude prevent her from becoming assertive and independent. Record and reward her various physical achievements, such as tying her shoes, riding her bicycle by herself, or being able to stand on her head.

- Make it clear to your little girl that you love her and appreciate her accomplishments as well as her femininity, whether she wants to play with dolls or with trucks, whether she wants to play house or climb trees. She needs to realize that assertiveness and achievement are as important to women as they are to men just as boys need to realize that being caring and sensitive are important aspects of being a man. Examine your perceptions about women in your family. Think about strong women you know and what you admire in them.

- Respect your daughter's individuality, and remember that there is more than one path to self-fulfillment. Despite active encouragement by you and your wife, she simply may not want to play with trucks or climb trees. Encourage achievement, but value your daughter's individuality and don't try to force her onto a career path while she is still a child. Many women establish their femininity with a husband and children before they feel like pursuing a career. On the other hand, many women want to finish their education and establish themselves in a successful career before becoming wives and mothers.

- Make it clear to your children that you respect their mother as a competent person. Be supportive of her goals, both inside or outside the home, and let your children know that competence is what counts in either area.

MORALITY AND YOUR CHILDREN

In Europe, a woman is near death from cancer. One drug might save her, a form of radium that a druggist in the same town had recently discovered. The druggist was charging $2,000, ten times what the drug cost him to make. The sick woman's husband, Heinz, went to everyone he knew to borrow the money, but he could only get together about half of what it cost. He told the druggist that his wife was dying and asked him to sell it cheaper or let him pay later, but the druggist said no. The husband got desperate and broke in to the man's store to steal the drug for his wife. Should the husband have done that? Why?

By posing dilemmas like this and asking children questions about them, psychologist Lawrence Kohlberg put together a six-stage theory of moral development that helps explain how and when our children learn right from wrong.[9] His theory, like Piaget's, is based on mental development, but it is not as strictly tied to age. During the first two stages, children are said to be premoral. They have no concept of good or bad. Infants, for example, simply try to avoid pain or seek pleasure. A young child in the first stage of moral development is likely to think: I should not hit the baby because I will get a spanking. Gradually, by the time they are two or three, children move into the second stage in which behavior is based on rewards. They learn to be good in order to get a reward instead of to avoid punishment. This stage is purely egocentric and reflects no real understanding of right or wrong.

During the next two stages, children learn what Kohlberg calls conventional morality. Stage 3 is the "good boy, good girl" stage in which four- to six-year-olds want to be good to avoid your disapproval. They want to please other people and be considered good children. Stage 4 is the "law and order" stage, during which children usually develop a great respect for authority and the value of rules. Seven-year-olds know how to play cops and robbers. They insist that the rules of Monopoly are law and cannot be changed. The tendency of children to obey rules at this stage appears to be more than a desire to avoid punishment. It seems to be related to a true belief in society's rules and a desire to preserve the social order, even in the games they play.

Through these four stages, according to Kohlberg, morality means following the rules of society. The fifth and sixth stages involve the development of a set of personal moral principles rather than blind acceptance of the rules of society or authority figures. During the fifth stage, moral action is considered in relation to individual rights and standards of behavior set up by society. People who reach this stage obey the law not because they want to avoid punishment or receive a reward but because they do not want to lose the respect of society and do not want to be thought of as immoral. The sixth and most advanced stage involves morality of principles and conscience. At this stage, abstract ethical principles (i.e., the golden rule, the sacred nature of human life, and the ultimate values of the individual) are used to guide behavior. People who reach this stage follow their principles in order to avoid self-condemnation ("I couldn't live with myself if I did that"). In other words, they have developed a true moral conscience and understanding of right and wrong.

Some people reach this final level by adolescence, but many never achieve it at all. They seem to get stuck at a lower level. You probably know people who obsequiously obey police or their bosses in order to please them (stage 3) or who declare that they do everything by the book (stage 5). But even people who have reached the highest level of moral functioning may occasionally do things because they want approval or because they fear authority.

Kohlberg's theory is not supported by all researchers. There are questions, for instance, about whether or not the stages are the same for each child or in each culture. There is no question, however, about the importance of moral development, and Kohlberg's outline is one way to help us understand how our children think and how we can help them reach the highest levels of moral thinking.

Researchers have found that mothers, because they usually spend much more time with children, play a more important role in the moral development of their children than do fathers. They also found, however, that fathers who are closely involved in indicating morally and socially acceptable behavior and who are also affectionate and attentive to their children's needs seem to be particularly good models for moral development. Children of such fathers score high on measures of moral judgment and values and are likely to imitate their father's socially responsible behavior. The quality of your relationship with your children has an especially strong influence on whether or not they take responsibility for their own actions and have a well-developed conscience. Boys and girls who have a warm relationship with a competent father who is actively committed to them are likely to be responsible sons and daughters.[10] It's as if you were looking over their shoulders even when you aren't there to tell them how to behave. And moral development works both ways. If you are a caring father, you will probably find yourself adjusting your own behavior in order to set a good example for your children. You are likely to think twice before running a stop light or getting drunk and abusive in front of your children.

To be a nurturing dad who contributes positively to his children's moral development you can do the following:

- Be an authoritative father without being authoritarian. An authoritative father is one who can provide guidance in what is right but who also allows some leeway for his children's opinions. An authoritarian father is one who dictates morality to his children. This may force them into submission, but it does not help them develop their own sense of right and wrong.
- Tell your children exactly how you expect them to behave and why. Explain the moral principles behind what you expect of them, and discuss the moral implications of your own as well as their behavior. The kinds of moral decisions you and your wife make may often be quite different, but each of you is likely to have a special perspective that will influence your children. Explain exactly how you reach certain ethical decisions, and make the steps involved in your deliberations as clear as possible so they can follow similar steps in their own decision making. But remember that no matter how often or how thoroughly you explain things, your children are more likely to do what you do than what you say.
- Remember that moral development is a gradual process. Don't expect a three-year-old to have the same understanding of right and wrong as the typical six- or eight-year-old. Instead, encourage moral development by showing your children moral behavior that may be above their current level of understanding. They may not immediately understand why you would give food and clothes to a homeless person, but they may recall your compassion and follow your example as they grow older.

- In many instances you will be your children's first policeman, judge, and boss, so be careful to teach them how to deal with and respect authority. But do not insist that they rigidly conform to the demands of adults. Explain the importance of mutual respect in any relationship, but let your children know that authority figures can make mistakes.

DISCIPLINING YOUR CHILDREN

You are well on the way to producing a well-rounded little person, one who is assertive and sensitive, one who is self-confident and eager for greater achievements, one who has the makings of a morally responsible adult. Don't throw it all away by being an excessively punitive father. You weren't perfect. Don't expect to have a perfect child. You may have a beaming beauty who wakes up every morning with a smile and is a pleasure to be with all day. You may have a moody monster who's never happy and always ready to give you a fight. More likely, you'll have a child who is somewhere between those extremes, one who is perfect sometimes, not so perfect other times, one who is good at some things, not so good at others. Biology sets the tone and gives each child a specific endowment and temperament from birth. But what happens after that, especially during childhood, is strongly influenced by you and your wife. You can take much of the credit or blame for how your child behaves. And one of the most important ways you influence your child is through discipline or the lack of it.

Unfortunately, too many parents, both mothers and fathers, equate discipline with punishment—physical punishment. Surveys indicate that nearly half of all parents believe that corporal punishment is wrong and ineffective, but the same surveys indicate that more than 80 percent of parents do spank their children on occasion.[11] Traditional discipline and physical punishment, however, are not the best way to teach children right from wrong. If you are an effective father, punishment may not be involved at all in your relationship with your children. It is your job to teach your children right from wrong, but this does not give you the right to deprive them of their basic human rights. They should have the right to express their feelings, make choices, and to have a sense of control.

- Teach your children right from wrong by your own behavior. Make sure you spend a lot of time with them so they can learn from your example. Make your expectations for appropriate behavior clear to them by your actions and words. Demonstrate confidence, independence, empathy, and high moral standards, and if you are a loving and caring father, they will learn from and follow your example. Concentrate on giving your children a hug or kiss for good behavior rather than a slap for bad behavior. Frequent use of physical punishment, whether with a belt, hairbrush, or the palm of your hand, shows your children that you think violence is acceptable behavior. Physical punishment may also reinforce the child's feeling that outside forces and not an internal conscience are supposed to govern their behavior.
- Consider both the short- and long-term goals when disciplining your children. Are you out for immediate conformity and control, or are you trying to shape your child's future behavior and independence? A toddler or preschooler can usually be intimidated or pressured into doing what you say, but if you are trying to encourage internal moral standards, independent think-

ing, and self-discipline, the best teacher is your own good example.

- Let your children know when they have done something wrong by telling them why you disapprove, not by smacking them. If you are a loving and loved father, your disapproval of a child's behavior can be one of the best forms of discipline. Don't simply tell a young child to be good. Explain in detail what you mean and be specific about what you expect. Tell the child why it is not right to hurt others or to destroy property. Your three- or five-year-old or even your ten-year-old doesn't know all the rules and can't be expected to obey them unless you explain them. Children cannot develop a value system in a vacuum.

- If a child loses control and continues to misbehave, even after your patient explanation, be firm. Tell the child to sit down and be quiet or to go into another room and cool off for a while. Avoid a power struggle, and give the child a chance to calm down without putting too much emphasis on the bad behavior. Give the child space and do not repeatedly criticize the bad behavior. Instead, praise your child for regaining self-control and focus on the child's good behavior as much as possible.

- Having a child sit down or go into another room for a few minutes should be explained as an opportunity for the child to think about the consequences of his or her behavior and ways to avoid that behavior in the future. It should be seen as a time out or cooling-off period after a frustrating situation. Don't expect to turn a brat into an angel all at once. Aim for gradual improvements in behavior. They will come as your child grows older, begins to act less impulsively, and develops the ability to think about the consequences of his or her behavior.

- When your children do something wrong, let them know about it in a constructive way. Focus on the behavior, not the child. Explain why pulling the cat's tail is not a good thing to do instead of telling your child that he or she is bad, stupid, or vicious. This kind of generalized criticism will undermine any child's self-confidence. Express your disappointment, but let your child know that you believe the misbehavior was only a temporary failing. In order to live up to your positive expectations, the child is more likely to avoid irresponsible or hurtful behavior in the future.

- The best way to get children to do what you want—pick up their toys, get ready for bed—is to reward them for their good behavior, especially if the reward comes immediately after the job is done. And the reward doesn't have to be candy or toys. Reward your child with your attention. Make a game out of putting toys away (Who can fill up a box with blocks first?) or brushing teeth (Let's see whose teeth can get the whitest). In the long run, your loving attention will be much more effective in shaping your child's behavior than any amount of spankings, admonitions, threats, or even toys and candy.

- Resist the urge to use physical punishment. Many parents still see spanking and other forms of physical punishment as nothing more than good old discipline. Others don't agree but sometimes give in to urges to slap or hit out of frustration. But even if you mean well, hitting children is not an effective teaching tool and definitely not any way to demonstrate appropriate behavior. "Spare the rod and spoil the child" is probably the most destructive adage ever uttered. It may come from the Bible, but it comes from a time in the history of childhood that we don't want to repeat. An indication that the history of childhood still has a long way to go can be seen in Germany, where the children's commission of the parliament even wants to pass a law making "spanking, boxing ears, withholding affection, constant nagging, or threatening children with the bogeyman" illegal.[12] If you ever find yourself excessively punishing your child, seek help from a clergy person, family doctor, psychologist, or other professional.

- Remember that children want and need your attention and will go to great lengths—even risk a spanking—to get it. Many parents say "This'll hurt me more than it hurts you," and they are right. Most parents who admit spanking their children also admit feeling extremely guilty afterward and take the blame for the incident, saying that it was their frustration, not the child's behavior, that caused the incident. Unfortunately, the spanking coupled with the guilt can encourage repeated bad behavior. The embarrassed and sorry parent immediately hugs the just-spanked child, begs forgiveness, and, in effect, rewards the child for misbehaving. Many children, especially those who don't get a lot of loving attention, quickly learn that a good way to get attention or to get a reward is to misbehave.

- Don't think that because you were beaten or abused as a child that you are condemned to pass on that behavior to your children. Numerous studies indicate that abuse does tend to beget abuse but need not always. A review of these studies suggests that only about 30 percent of people who were abused as children are abusive as parents. This is six times higher than the rate for the general population, but it also indicates that the vicious circle can be stopped. If you were hit as a child, remember how it felt and resolve not to inflict such pain on your own children.[13]

- Encourage your wife to avoid using physical punishment when the children misbehave. She probably spends more time with the children than you do and is more likely to get frustrated and strike out. If you are closely involved in disciplining the children and if you support her, she will have fewer discipline problems and be less likely to resort to physical punishment.
- Don't even threaten physical punishment. You may get temporary obedience, but you won't be teaching the child anything positive. Depending on their temperament, children who are subjected to repeated physical discipline are likely to end up as either excessively submissive or unthinkingly rebellious.
- If you need some sort of physical release in the face of a frustrating child, remember that it's better to stamp your foot, bang a table, or kick a chair than to risk harming your child. You may be sorely tempted to slap a child who sasses you or shake the daylights out of one who breaks a lamp, but it is important that you teach your children that hitting is not how a mature adult communicates displeasure.
- Don't resort to emotional or verbal abuse. Don't say "I won't love you if you don't . . ." Such threats, like physical punishment, undermine a child's sense of emotional security and confidence and can lead to overly dependent behavior.

REFERENCES

1. de Mause, L., *The History of Childhood*. New York: Harper and Row, 1975.

2. Reuter, M., and Biller, H., Perceived Paternal Nurturance-Availability in Personality Adjustment Among College

Males, *Journal of Consulting and Clinical Psychology*, Vol. 40, 1973, p. 339.

3. Rutherford, E., and Mussen, P., Generosity in Nursery School Boys, *Child Development*, Vol. 39, 1968, p. 755.

4. McClelland, D., et al., Making It to Maturity, *Psychology Today*, June 1978, p. 98.

5. Franz, C., McClelland, D., and Weinberger, J., Childhood Antecedents of Conventional Social Accomplishment in Midlife Adults, *Journal of Social Psychology*, vol. 60, 1991, p. 586.

6. Lytton, H., "Discipline Encounters Between Young Boys and Their Mothers and Fathers: Is There a Contingency System?" *Developmental Psychology*, Vol. 15, 1979, p. 256.

7. McLeod, B., "Once A Bully, Always . . . ," *Psychology Today*, July 1985, p. 19.

8. Horner, M., in J. Bardwich et al. (Eds.), *Feminine Personality and Conflict*. Monterey, CA: Brooks/Cole, 1972.

9. Kohlberg, L. *The Philosophy of Moral Development*. New York: Harper and Row, 1981.

10. Biller, H., and Solomon, R., *Child Maltreatment and Paternal Deprivation: A Manifesto for Research, Prevention and Treatment*. Lexington, MA: Lexington Books D.C. Heath, 1986.

11. Stark, E., Spanking Kids for the Wrong Reasons, *Psychology Today*, January 1985, p. 16.

12. "Hug Your Kids Today—Or Else," *Washington Post*, p. A1, December 2, 1992.

13. Rosenfeld, A., "Does Abuse Beget Abuse?" *Psychology Today*, August 1987, p. 9.

SUGGESTED READINGS

TEACHING CHILDREN SELF-DISCIPLINE by Gordon, T., Times Books, 1989.

BRINGING UP A MORAL CHILD: TEACHING YOUR CHILD TO BE KIND, JUST AND RESPONSIBLE by Schulman, M. and McKler, E., Addison-Wesley, 1985.

THE MORAL LIFE OF CHILDREN by Coles, R., Houghton Mifflin, 1986.

PLAYFUL PARENTING: TURNING THE DILEMMA OF DISCIPLINE INTO FUN AND GAMES by Weston, D. and Weston, M., Tarcher/Perigee, 1993.

Schooling the Mind and Body

Margaret Mead grew up in a world that expected women to do little more than make babies and bake pies, but she also grew up in a family of academics who valued education and intellectual achievement and gave her the confidence to look beyond those barriers imposed by society. Mead took her intellectual heritage and academic background and marched right to the top of her profession. She was a world-famous anthropologist by the time she was thirty and became one of the most visible, if sometimes controversial, scientists of her day.

In her autobiography, she wrote, "In school I always felt that I was different, set apart in a way that could not be attributed to any gift I had, but only to my background . . . to the explicit academic interests of my parents".[1] Her father was a professor at the University of Pennsylvania in the Wharton School of Finance and Commerce, and family life revolved around academic and university matters. At home, Mead remembers being exposed to a continuous running commentary on schools and education.

In addition to a respect for education, Mead learned how to think from her father. "I greatly respected the way my father thought," she said. "He taught me the importance of thinking clearly and of keeping one's premises clear." His enormous respect for facts made his academic work rigorous. His vivid accounts of how a street railway in Massachusetts had failed and of the fate of a pretzel factory gave her a sense of the way theory and practice must be related, of how important it is to link together the concrete and the abstract.

Mead attributed much of her academic success to the early influences of her parents, particularly her father. The first thing she got from them was a set of genes and a unique pattern of potential intellectual abilities. She learned to think like her academically oriented parents and pushed herself even beyond their achievements. Your children, too, are likely to inherit intellectual abilities similar to your own and to think like you do. In fact, the best predictor of your child's academic performance is your own and your wife's intelligence. Studies of identical twins and adopted children indicate that intelligence has a strong genetic basis. Identical twins separated at birth and reared in completely different types of families have been found to be remarkably similar intellectually as adults. But genes are only the starting point. It's what you give your children after they are born that greatly influences what they do with their genetic inheritance.

Researchers have found that loving, nurturing fathers tend to have preschool children who are above average in social and intellectual abilities. Restrictive fathers who are constantly telling their children to sit down and be quiet are not encouraging independence and achievement.[2] As children enter their school years, a father's closeness continues to have a positive influence on their grades and achievement-test scores.[3] But don't be fooled into thinking that IQ and achievement tests are all there is to intelligence. These tests do pretty well at predicting success in school because they adequately measure necessary skills—a child's ability to communicate and understand language. Standardized tests do not, however, measure other major components of intelligence, such as problem solving, social skills, and creativity—abilities necessary to do well in the real world. It is important to encourage your children to do well in school, but it is equally important for you to encourage the whole spectrum of their individual intellectual abilities.

TEACHING YOUR CHILDREN PROBLEM SOLVING

Margaret Mead's mother put her academic career on hold in order to tackle the challenges that come with rearing children and managing a home. Her father focused his problem-solving abilities on the university and business worlds. Young Margaret learned a great deal from each of them, and your children will learn a great deal from you and your wife. But they will learn different things from each of you. You and your wife have different responsibilities and interests, different jobs inside and outside your home, and your children will see how you approach and solve the problems you encounter, whether it be hooking up the videocassette recorder (VCR) or making an omelet.

What are some of the ways you can help?

- Be your children's first teacher. You don't have to be a college professor or even a high school graduate to stimulate your children's intellectual and problem-solving abilities. Let them learn by sharing in even routine chores, which you may hate but which they will find fascinating. There's a whole physics lesson in a broken toaster, a biology lesson in a broken egg. Take advantage of such natural learning opportunities. Explain what you are doing, the use of various household objects and tools, and why you are choosing a particular method to solve a problem. Let your child help by fetching materials or by actually doing part of the job.

- Remember that different children have different styles of learning and different ways of relating to their environment. Some learn best from watching and imitating others, some do best when allowed to master new materials on their own. If you have been closely involved in watching your child's mind develop, you will know what kind of learning opportunities best suit his or her needs and intellectual style.

- Encourage your children to be involved in your decision-making processes as you do various things around the house. Ask them for advice, respond to their suggestions, and be supportive of their ideas. If they come up with good ideas, use them. If their ideas aren't especially helpful, you have a chance to explain why and do a little teaching.

- Share your decision-making process with your children. Mulling over the financial advantages and disadvantages of getting a new car versus taking a vacation may help you clarify your priorities as well as give your children insights into real-life problem-solving situations.
- Be patient with your little helpers. Problem solving involves perseverance, and your children can learn from watching you stick to a job until it is done. Encourage your children to be patient and take pride in getting things done.
- If there are jobs that you can't or don't want to do, let your children learn from watching someone who can. Call a neighbor or friend for help if you can't program your VCR. Your clever children, who probably love television, may even learn to do it and take over that awesome responsibility.
- Expose your children to all sorts of expert thinkers and problem solvers. In his autobiography, Benjamin Franklin described in detail how his father took him for walks to see various types of artisans in action and how he exposed Young Ben to his conversations with business, civic, and religious leaders. These excursions undoubtedly contributed to the development of Franklin's wide-ranging intellectual accomplishments.
- Share in your children's hobbies, but don't do everything for them. Let your children help build a tree house or a doll house, even if it means a few bent nails or wasted pieces of wood. It is more important for your children to take pride in contributing to the finished product than to have a perfect product. Whether it be a garden, a puzzle, or a tree house, any father–child project can be a very rewarding experience for fathers and children.
- Remember that your children's interests may not al-

ways be the same as yours. Even if you don't particularly care about sports, stamp collections, or the latest adventures of the X-MEN, try to show some interest. You may even learn something. Be supportive of your children's hobbies and take an interest. Think of it as a chance to learn something along with your children. Even if you don't get directly involved, let your children know that you support and appreciate their attempts to reach out and learn new things.

- Stimulate your children's intellectual development by playing games with them. And you don't have to wait until they are old enough to master checkers or chess to use games to teach strategy planning and problem solving. Babies can learn how to stack blocks or find hidden toys. As they grow older, you can graduate from Candyland to Monopoly, Scrabble, and card games. Besides teaching a child how to analyze certain situations, these kinds of games are a great way to encourage an interest in words and numbers.

- Remember that boys and girls tend to have different inborn intellectual capabilities and that your unconscious sexist attitudes shove boys and girls in different directions. Because boys tend to be better at math than girls, for example, many men reward and encourage mathematical thinking more in their sons than in their daughters. Be aware of this bias, and remember that your daughters may need your support and encouragement even more than your sons in order to develop their mathematical talents.

- Help your children broaden their language skills by talking to them about your job and your interests. Many of them will be different from those of your wife, as will the way you express yourself. You will introduce your children to a different vocabulary and a different way of expressing themselves. Talk about your work, sports, literature, whatever interests you that can contribute to your child's growing store of words and knowledge.

FOSTERING THE CREATIVE SPIRIT IN YOUR CHILDREN

Creativity is the spice of the intellect. It involves the imaginative joining of thoughts or things never before connected to produce new solutions to old problems. Creativity is one of the most prized aspects of intelligence, as important in science, sports, and social interactions as it is in the arts or literature. But like problem solving, it is not measured very well by standard intelligence tests. Researchers have, however, devised ways to measure and stimulate certain aspects of creativity. The focus in these measures is on divergent thinking, the ability to give more than one answer to a question or to generate several solutions to a problem. For instance, a child may be asked how many uses there are for a paper hanger or how many objects can be represented by a particular geometric shape. The most creative children produce the most—and the most original—answers.

Research with creative children suggests that fathers play a particularly important role in fostering creativity in their daughters; mothers, in their sons. A close relationship with the parent of the other sex seems to be especially useful in helping creative children overcome gender stereotypes that might keep them from thinking or behaving creatively. And a close relationship with two loving and supportive parents is likely to give children an even broader range of knowledge and thinking styles so important in generating creative ideas.

- Encourage your children to think and act independently. Allow them to question authority and the traditional ways of doing things. Help them understand that there is more than one way to look at a situation or a problem and let them feel free to search for and try out new and different perspectives.
- Encourage creativity by showing respect for your children's comments, ideas, questions, and preferences. Let them try out their ideas. Don't simply tell them how things must be done.
- When tackling household problems, sit down before you start and ask your child how many ways the job can be done. How many ways can you get a large rug into a room or remove water from a flooded basement? Let your child help you rearrange the furniture in a room. Encourage him or her to visualize different ways the furniture can be arranged and think about what each plan means in terms of convenience, practicality, and attractiveness.
- Play games like twenty questions that stimulate your child's imagination. Let your child imagine being an animal, person, object, event, place, or even an abstract concept as you ask more and more focused questions. Then you do the imagining and let your child ask the questions.
- Give your children room to be creative. Set aside a place where they can let their imagination run wild. Make it a special place where they know they can do what they want without worrying about neatness or rules (within certain limits, of course). Give them a large space on which to draw, perhaps a wall covered with plastic or some washable material. Add shelves, a workbench, tables and chairs, and other things to experiment and play with. Even if it is just a large closet or a divided off portion of a room or yard, make

it a special place where children will feel free to do whatever they can imagine.

- Help your children overcome any social pressures that might interfere with their attempts at creativity. This is especially important during the third and fourth and seventh and eighth grades when other children may inhibit your children's creativity. During the third and fourth grades, cliques—usually all boy or all girl—begin to form, and children may be extremely sensitive about doing anything that might damage their image with their friends. A boy who has been making great strides with his piano lessons may begin to slack off if he feels that his buddies think he is a sissy. A girl who likes to build and fly model airplanes or do chemistry experiments may retreat to the doll house if she thinks her friends don't see her as feminine. During the seventh and eighth grades, as they grow more interested in the other sex, gender stereotypes can again interfere with creativity. But if your children are confident of your approval of their creative efforts, they are likely to resist pressures to conform.

- Don't let your own gender dictate the types of creativity you encourage in your children. Encourage a broad range of talents in children of both sexes. Gender differences have little to do with a child's ability to do most complex tasks. Girls may draw and paint more accurately because of greater fine muscle control, but boys may be better able to reproduce three-dimensional drawings because of superior spatial perception. But neither ability makes boys or girls naturally better artists. Any girl or boy may have great artistic, mechanical, mathematical, verbal, or other talents that need your support if they are to develop fully.

- Teach your children to be creative in their social life. Role playing, for example, is a good way to help a child come up with creative solutions to problems with a bully, teacher, or friend. Act out the problem with your child and see how many ways you and your child can come up with to deal with it or to solve it.

HELPING YOUR CHILDREN THROUGH SCHOOL

As your children advance through the grade school years, formal education becomes a major focus of their lives. But just because they are going to school doesn't mean your job as teacher is over. Our elementary schools teach the three R's, but they don't do it equally well for all children. Grade school discriminates first against boys, then against girls. Girls learn to read more quickly than boys and are generally better behaved than boys. Four to five times as many boys as girls have difficulty with reading, and because they are typically more aggressive and active than girls, they are more likely to be disruptive in class. And because reading well and sitting still in class are important in the early grades, girls usually do better in those grades. But as boys and girls grow older, the situation changes. Most boys catch up in reading by the time they are ten or twelve, and their assertiveness may become an asset in getting the teacher's attention. Girls are more likely to be rebuked for calling out and are expected to be more passive and ladylike in the classroom.[4]

One of the reasons elementary schools discriminate against young boys is that most schools are dominated by women, with a ratio of female to male teachers at about six to one—and more than fifty to one in the first few grades. Because of this, many boys begin to see school and intellectual achievement as feminine endeavors. This is especially true for boys who do not have a close relationship with a father who values education.

They may see the teacher as just another controlling female and rebel against her in an effort to assert themselves in the presence of women. The teacher, feeling threatened, increases her efforts to control such a boy, and the stressful relationship that develops contributes to an already existing bias against boys in school. Boys tend to be more naturally disruptive and get many more warnings and scoldings than girls. There are also indications that many teachers give girls better grades than boys, even those who may have performed just as well but not as quietly.

Young girls are, on average, more advanced than boys when they enter school and are much less likely to have learning disabilities, but this is only part of the explanation for why so many more boys have difficulties with reading. In general, teachers react less favorably toward boys than girls during reading lessons and tend to allow them less oral reading time. In addition, because girls have a same-sex adult model who is a highly competent reader, they tend to be more interested in reading and attach more prestige to it.

Despite such disadvantages, in different circumstances, most boys can learn to read as well as girls. When children are given programmed, independent reading instruction, boys and girls do about equally well. But when children are taught in small reading groups with a female teacher, girls do better. In Germany, where elementary school teachers are usually men and reading is considered a masculine talent, boys have significantly better reading scores than girls and are less likely to suffer from severe reading problems.

Although the form of discrimination may be different, girls as well as boys can also be victims of the biases of the elementary school classroom. Girls tend to be more sensitive to the attitudes of others and especially to the prejudices of authority figures. Accordingly, their independence, assertiveness, and motivation for achievement can be inhibited by traditional female teachers. Although female teachers usually react more negatively to young boys, the overall elementary school atmosphere may subtly downgrade the importance of long-term achievement for girls. Despite the number of female teachers, for example, women tend not to be well represented in school administrations. A girl's impression of the school bureaucracy may also bruise her pride because female teachers are usually working under the supervision of a male principal.

Having a supportive, encouraging male teacher early in the elementary school years can be as important for girls as for boys. If a girl has been exposed only to female teachers and has never had an adult male show her that he values learning and achievement as a natural feminine characteristic, she may find it more difficult to assert herself intellectually as she grows into adolescence and adulthood. Without such early self-confidence, she is likely to take the path of least resistance when faced with restrictive gender stereotypes.

A major remedy to the feminized classroom would be to have more men teach in the early elementary school grades. This is not something over which you have much control, but there are many ways you can insert your maleness into your children's education and even into the school system.

- Get to know your children's teachers and become a full partner in the education process by making time to sit in on some of your children's classes. For the most part, mothers deal with the schools, and most schools are more prepared to deal with mothers than fathers. Mothers typically communicate their concerns to the schools, and mothers are the ones who are usually contacted by the teacher if there is a problem. Overcome this bias by visiting the school, meeting with the teachers, and showing them that you are just as concerned as your wife is about your children's education. In fact, you may be in a better position than your wife to understand the problems of the feminized classroom and the need for more male input.

- Push for your child to have some regular contact with a male teacher during the early elementary school years. If this isn't possible, suggest that the school could benefit from a program that brings parents into the classroom. An accountant could give a lesson in basic budgeting, a pilot could lecture on the fundamentals of flying, an insurance agent could explain the nature of actuarial practices. Remember that it is important to have women as well as men describe their jobs to children and help overcome sex-role stereotypes about educational and career opportunities.

- Remember that being a competent parent doesn't just mean going to PTA meetings and talking to teachers. Some children whose fathers never talk to a teacher or visit the school are very happy and competent students. But you should encourage your child's school-related activities. Pay close attention to your children's homework assignments and make sure they get done properly and on time. Your close involvement lets your children see that you value learning and education.

- Don't worry that you won't understand phonics or the new math. You may learn something along with your children or at least get to brush up on some long forgotten skills.

- Don't do your children's homework for them. If they need help with a difficult assignment, work through it with them, making sure they understand the process and learn how to get to the final answer. Encourage your children by asking focused, step-by-step questions.

- Take the time to answer all of your child's questions. Don't just emphasize the answer. Consider the form of the question and compliment your child for asking a difficult question or one that gets to the heart of the matter. Asking questions, even some that seem simple, is a crucial step in acquiring knowledge.

- Don't be afraid to admit that you can't answer a particular question. Help your child find the answer. Go to the encyclopedia or dictionary or wherever and encourage your child by expressing your interest in finding the answer.

- Talk to your children about your responsibilities and what you do at work and establish a two-way pattern of communication. If you have a history of rapport with your children, they will be more likely to talk to you about what they are doing in school and about any problems they are having. If you don't know where the problems lie, you won't be able to help solve them.

- While helping your children with their homework, examine your basic attitudes toward education. If you had a difficult time with school, don't hesitate to talk about your experiences. Encourage your child to achieve in all subjects, not just the ones in which you did well.

- Don't let homework become a battleground. Don't threaten or punish your children for efforts that don't meet your standards. Express your concern and let your children know that you expect them to do better on future assignments. With positive encouragement, they will try to meet a loving father's expectations.

- Don't let school and homework become so important that academic success is your child's only basis for self-esteem. Some children just aren't that interested in academic achievement or simply cannot keep up with their classmates. Special tutoring or summer school may be necessary, but remember that your child's basic self-acceptance is far more important than his or her success in school. Be supportive of your children's abilities and attempts to do their best whether or not they result in straight A's.

- Don't let schoolwork be the focus of your child's life. Don't hesitate to speak up when you think your child is being overloaded with homework. Find out if it really contributes to your child's understanding or is simply busywork. Talk to the teacher if you think your child may be getting too much pressure at school.

- Be aware of your children's other commitments. They may have religious training, sports activities, music lessons, and other afterschool activities that you and they consider important. But make sure that your children aren't so overscheduled that they don't have free time for spontaneous play. It is your job to teach your children how to schedule their time.

- Make sure your children know how important a good education will be in their lives. Explain how your education affected your career and your family finances. Explain how it is related to your ability to appreciate art, literature, and music and your other interests. But the best way to encourage your children's interest in such things is by your actions rather than what you say about the importance of education.

- Take your children on field trips. They probably love going on field trips with their schoolmates, but a personal adventure with you can have an even more lasting impression. You know your children's interests, level of understanding, and personality much better than does a teacher who has to deal with twenty to thirty youngsters. Don't limit your outings to zoos, museums, and places like Disneyland. A camping trip or visit to a bustling construction site or even to the town dump can be just as educational and just as much fun and will make your child feel special. One of your roles as an at-home teacher is to introduce your children to as many new learning opportunities as possible.

- Don't be sexist with regard to your children's education. Many parents think boys do well in math because they have natural ability, and parents and teachers often encourage boys more than girls to do well in math and science because they think science education is more important for boys than girls in terms of career and general knowledge. Margaret Mead's parents knew that wasn't true and so should you.

- Remember that your daughter's education is just as important as your son's and that your attitude will have a great deal to do with her intellectual development. Girls who do poorly in school often have neglectful, abusive, or hostile fathers. But even less destructive forms of fathering can interfere with a girl's educational achievements. For example, a loving father who encourages passivity, timidity, and dependency in his daughter is giving her mixed messages. Sometimes he may encourage competence, but other times he may appear uncomfortable about a daughter doing too well in areas that he considers to be masculine. An overly affectionate and solicitous father is likely to foster dependence rather than competence.

- Don't try to solve all of your daughter's problems for her. You will inhibit her independence and self-sufficiency. Girls who do well in both reading and math usually have fathers who consistently praise and reward their intellectual efforts. Studies have shown that outstanding female mathematicians often have especially close relationships with their fathers. If you are a highly accessible and interested father but allow your daughter autonomy and space to develop her skills, you will be an important factor in her intellectual development.

- Don't be a report card father. Don't ignore your children's education until they come home with a bad report card. Fathers who only get involved when there appears to be a problem often get into a cycle of bribing, cajoling, and demanding better grades. Such a father may even help his children with their homework for a few nights, but within a week or so he is likely to be preoccupied with his own interests until it is report card time again. Report card fathers may think they are doing their job, but by paying attention only when there is a problem, they are actually rewarding their children for doing poorly.

- Don't stop reading to your kids like many fathers do when their children learn to read. Take turns reading and letting them read to you. Show them by example that you find reading both important and enjoyable. Keep a lot of books and magazines around the house and let them see you reading—whether it's the newspaper, *Sports Illustrated,* a good novel, or something related to your work. Your support of reading and learning will be at least as important to your children's intellectual and educational attainments as is the quality of their school. In a study of 70,000 high school students in nine countries, educational researcher Alan Purves and his colleagues found that the home is the most important factor in children's involvement in reading. They found that the number of books and magazines in a child's home was a better indicator of that child's academic achievement than was family's income or educational level.[5]

- Take your kids to the library. Get them library cards as soon as they are old enough and let books become an important part of their lives. Do not, however, force children to read what you think they should read. Let them read at their own level about things that interest them. As their love of reading grows, their horizons will widen—from comic books to wherever their inquiring minds will take them.
- One way to encourage your children's interest in books is to let them know that you will let them stay up late to read but not to watch television.

EXERCISE AND PHYSICAL DEVELOPMENT

"Looking back, my memories of learning precise skills, memorizing long stretches of poetry, and manipulating paper are interwoven with memories of running—running in the wind, running through meadows, and running along country roads. . . ." Margaret Mead was a small but active child whose physical stamina complimented her intellectual pursuits and was essential to them. Her mentors and professors protested that women weren't strong enough to endure the rigors of jungle treks and the privations of life among native cultures, but Mead's field trips to Samoa, Manus, Bali, and New Guinea proved them wrong.

A healthy body was as important to Mead's success as was her lively intellect, and you should encourage physical fitness and competence as much as possible in your sons and daughters. In the first place, it will be important to their future health. A major study of more than 3,000 grade school through high school children found that those who were at least twenty pounds overweight by the time they reached high school were more likely than their lean classmates to have heart disease, arthritis, and other health problems as adults even if they later lost their excess weight as adults.[6] Then there is the problem of self-esteem and social acceptance. Body image becomes increasingly important as children near adolescence and grow more sensitive to how they look. Girls may worry that their breasts and hips are too large or too small. Boys may be particularly embarrassed if they are shorter or weaker than their friends. Their worries aren't unfounded. Overweight, underweight, awkward, and otherwise physically "different" children are likely to be rejected and ridiculed by other children. The best way to help your children avoid these problems is to encourage good health and physical fitness and to help them develop a sense of pride in their bodies.

Women are much more physically active and fitness-minded than they were a generation ago, but your attitude toward physical fitness is still likely to be different than that of your wife. From the time they were infants, you probably played more roughly with your children and put more emphasis on physical prowess, especially in your sons. You are probably more likely to tolerate your children playing rough-and-tumble games and to put a premium on athletic ability. These differences in attitude and behavior are likely to have an important impact on your children's physical development and sense of pride in their bodies.

- Set a good example for your children. The most important thing you can do to help your children become physically fit and develop a healthy body concept is to value your own body. If you are out of shape, do something about it. If you smoke or drink or eat too much, do something about it. You don't have to jog or work out or otherwise get involved in sports to excess, but you should take care of your health and physical fitness and show your children how important it is that they do the same.

■ You can't make your son taller or your daughter smaller, and you won't be able to overcome all the stereotypes society attaches to different body types. You can, however, encourage physical fitness and athletic competence in your sons and daughters. This will be relatively easy if you are athletic and sports-minded. And if your wife is fit and interested in physical activities, your children will have two quite different people to encourage fitness and athletic accomplishments. You and your children will probably enjoy shooting hoops, running races, swimming, ice skating, wrestling, and all sorts of physical activities together.

■ Take an active interest in your children's fitness and athletic endeavors. Even if you aren't a physical father, your children will take physical education classes at school and will probably be involved in some sort of athletic activities. Take time to applaud their efforts. Let them know that you value physical fitness and are as proud of their athletic accomplishments as you are of their intellectual gains. Take them to their coaching sessions, go to their games, encourage their increasing competence, and let them know that you feel it is important for them to be as physically fit and competent as their bodies allow. Let them know that success in athletics and intellectual endeavors can go together. A well-rounded boy or girl can feel just as comfortable on the playing field as in the library.

■ Don't have unrealistic expectations about your children's physical abilities. Encourage their accomplishments as they grow, but remember that some children mature more slowly than others. If they are healthy, their strength, speed, and coordination will show improvement throughout childhood and well into adolescence and adulthood. Boys usually gain in strength and speed during late childhood whereas girls typically taper off, especially if they are not involved in athletics. But it is as important for girls as it is for boys to develop a sense of pride in their bodies and their physical abilities. If your daughter is interested in sports, encourage her. As the main man in her life, you can show her that she can be admired for her femininity as well as for her athletic abilities.

- If your children are worried about their bodies or their appearance, boost their sense of confidence by talking about some of the physical concerns you had when you were younger and how you learned to cope with them. Were you worried about your big feet, short legs, or long neck? Explain to your children that these "defects" turned out to be less serious than they seemed at the time. Don't brush off a child's bodily concerns as frivolous by simply saying "You'll grow out of it." Be sympathetic to problems that are very real to your child.

- If your child is slow to mature, if he or she is short, clumsy, or overweight, treat it as you would a learning problem. Some children need extra help with reading, math, or other school subjects, others need extra help in their physical development. Working hard to overcome early disadvantages can build character, strengthen self-confidence, and be a good lesson in the persistence that will be needed to overcome many of life's problems.

- As your children grow, help them develop a solid sense of self-acceptance by helping them update their body image. Many once overweight, skinny, or ungainly adults continue to see themselves the way they once were and never get over the feeling of being physically inferior to others.

- Help your children develop a positive body image by fostering a pride in athletic competence, but do not put so much pressure on them that they don't enjoy the games they play. Provide support for your children to compete at an appropriate level so they have a chance to experience success. Encourage them to take pride in their current level of ability. Help them appreciate competition, self-improvement, and the joy of doing their best.

- Allow your children the freedom to choose their athletic interests. Don't pressure them into athletic competition because of your unfulfilled fantasies. Choices should be made on the basis of their interests and abilities, not yours. Sports can help your children mature physically, socially, and emotionally but only if they are practicing and performing because they want to, not because they feel pressured to earn your approval.

- Do not discourage children from getting involved in a particular sport or activity simply because of their size or body type, but do let them know that they might have to work harder than other children to overcome their size disadvantage and to overcome prejudices they may face because of their size.[7] With your support, children can develop the confidence and competence to surmount such things as size discrimination. Whether children are striving for respect for their opinions, social acceptance, a leadership role, or a spot on an athletic team, assertiveness in countering stereotypes is extremely important.

TV OR NOT TV?

Television is one of the greatest obstacles to physical fitness and intellectual development. Children who watch a lot of television (more than four hours a day) have been tested and found wanting. When compared with those who watch less than two hours a day, they are much more likely to be out of shape. They can do fewer push-ups, pull-ups, and sit-ups and score lower on overall measures of fitness.[8] This, of course, is not surprising. Sitting in front of the tube munching on all the junk food that gets advertised can interfere with more active pastimes and lead to lower levels of fitness. On the other hand, less physically fit children may prefer watching television to running around the yard. In either case, you have a vicious cycle. The passivity of television watching leads to poor physical fitness, which leads to more television watching.

Television is also a major problem in many homes with school-aged children because it is a highly seductive medium, and most youngsters would rather watch cartoons or MTV than read or do their homework. Despite the numerous arguments we hear about how television rots the brain and how worthless most television is, the couch potatoes seem to be winning the battle. Children watch, on average, twenty-five hours of television per week. Parents are guilty, too. According to the Institute for Social Research at the University of Michigan, television watching is the most popular leisure time activity shared by parents and children, accounting for about one-fourth of the time they spend together.[9]

Children do learn from what they see on TV. What they learn, of course, depends on what they watch. The real problem with this has more to do with the way we use television—whether we use it to bring the family together or to isolate family members. Some homes have several television sets, and parents and children go to separate rooms to watch their favorite shows. Some families watch television together but use it as an excuse to avoid communicating with each other.

What are some good ways to think about the advantages and disadvantages of TV?

- Remember that an enthusiastic offer by a father to play a game, read a book, or go for a walk is a much better way to unglue a child from the television than by simply unplugging it. If both you and your wife are closely involved with your children in a variety of activities, excessive television watching is much less likely.
- If you are worried about the example you set with television, don't keep a television in your bedroom. Don't keep the television on all the time. Don't use television as a baby-sitter. Establish reasonable television-watching habits for your children and yourself by limiting the amount of time and kinds of shows you and they watch.
- Make it clear to children that television is allowed only if chores, homework, and other jobs are done and done well. Give your children a chance to watch a special show if they have done their work.
- Remember that children are more influenced by what you do than what you say. Set specific limits on television for yourself and for your children. Use a TV guide to help teach your children to plan ahead, marking off a weekly schedule and discussing why you each want to watch certain programs. This kind of structured approach may not work in all families, but the important thing is to prevent television from becoming

the dominating force in your family. Television can be quite useful if it is kept in perspective.

- Talk back to your television. Your reactions to television programs can stimulate your child's learning by demonstrating the value of critical thinking. Discuss television news and editorials with your family and help your children realize that what they see on television isn't necessarily the whole story.
- Don't hesitate to be critical when you watch documentaries or other special programs. Talk about the contents and discuss how the program relates to your own life and family. Analyze the ploys behind commercials and particularly the flaws in logic contained in most advertisements.
- Treat home computers and computer games the same way you treat television. Use them to help your children learn, not as baby-sitters. Computer games can be educational, but don't let them detract from family life, and don't let them be for boys only as is the case in many families. Surveys continue to find that families with boys are much more likely to have home computers than are families with girls.[10]

INTRODUCING YOUR KIDS TO THE WORLD OF WORK

Margaret Mead didn't have television or computer games to play with. She had a family that put a premium on education and academic achievement. By the time she was seventeen, she said, "I was eager to enter the academic world for which all my life had prepared me." She entered it with gusto and fulfilled all her ambitions. She wrote eleven books, received twenty-seven honorary degrees, and helped shape the intellectual world in which she lived. Your sons and daughters may not grow up to be great scientists or even make great achievements in any particular intellectual arena, but the love of learning that you instill in them will be one of their most important tools as they develop into happy, well-adjusted adolescents and adults and head off to college or careers.

The love of learning you have fostered in your children is important, but you also have to help prepare them for the world of work. Near adolescence, they have to begin thinking about where, when, or whether to go to college. They have to begin thinking about jobs and careers, and in many ways their decisions will be influenced by you and your job. What you do at work may not be very visible to your children, but your job will affect their lives in more than a financial sense. What you do and how you feel about it helps determine what kind of father you are. If your success depends on assertiveness and independence, you will probably demonstrate these characteristics and encourage them in your children. If your job security is based on pleasing your boss, you may be more likely to value submissiveness and conformity. If you hate your job, you may not be fun to be with after a day on the job. If you love your job too much, you may be so preoccupied with it that you don't have enough time for your children and don't develop close relationships with them.

Instead of letting your job interfere with your role as a father, use it as another way to let your children get to know you. Your job is probably a major part of your life, and if your children don't see you at work or understand what you do, they may be missing out on an important part of who you are. Your job can also be an important way to teach your children about the world of work they will soon be entering.

Here are some ways to think about your job in terms of your children and their future working lives.

- Don't let your job overwhelm your family commitments. Many men feel that they can't be successful in a career as well as be a highly involved parent on a day-to-day basis. They then use this as an excuse to avoid sharing in parenting. It may be difficult to come home exhausted from a twelve-hour workday and be a good father, and it may be just as difficult to spend a great deal of time with your family and still be successful in a highly competitive career. Yet many extremely competent career women manage to find the time to be positively involved with their children every day, and you can do the same.
- Find a way to balance your commitments to fatherhood and your job. Decide exactly what you need to do to be a competent parent as well as get ahead in your career. This may mean working especially hard at the office but refusing to accept business calls at home. Or it may mean working through lunch in order to leave for home at the end of the day without a bulging briefcase. If you can find a good balance between work and family life, you are likely to be successful in both.
- If your wife works, encourage her career goals and do your share as a parent. When you and your wife contribute equally to your family life as well as encourage each other's careers, there is a much greater chance that both of you will be able to balance family and work commitments.
- Don't let your wife complain that what she really needs is a wife, not a husband. Remember that you have a commitment to your wife as well as to your job and children. Don't let the sometimes overwhelming de-

mands of career and fatherhood detract from your marriage.

- Take your children to work with you on occasion and let them see how Daddy makes a living. Don't be afraid that your children will embarrass you or that your supervisors or fellow employees will not want to be distracted by your children. They'll probably get a kick out of having your kids visit, at least for a while.
- If it isn't possible to have your children see you on the job, be sure to tell them all about your work. Show them pictures and explain your responsibilities. Help them find out as much as possible about a variety of occupations, especially as they grow older and begin to think about what they want to be.
- Take your children on business trips with you when possible. This will be exciting for them and give you a good chance to spend some special time with them. Don't be afraid to take your children out of school for a day to be with you at work or on the road. What they learn with you may be quite valuable—something they otherwise wouldn't get a chance to learn—and they can surely make up a missed day or two of school.
- Make sure your children know how to contact you at work and that they feel free to do so. It is very reassuring for children who come home from school to know that they can telephone their parents at work. You, too, will feel better knowing that your children can reach you even when you are at work.
- In addition to exposing your children to your career, you can also help prepare them for their future responsibilities. Encourage, but don't force, your children to seek out occasional part-time work. Cutting the lawn, shoveling the snow, baby-sitting, or having a paper route can help them develop a sense of responsibility

and learn the value of money, even in the elementary school years.

- Use your job as a jumping off point to discuss college, careers, and work with your children. Your job and your wife's will be their introduction to work. As your children near adolescence, help them find out about other jobs and college and career options. Be careful, however, about sex-role stereotypes. Some fathers tend to have limited views of their daughters' career options and blatantly limit their educational and career aspirations.

REFERENCES

1. Mead, M., *Blackberry Winter*. New York: William Morrow, 1972.

2. Radin, N., Father-Child Interaction and the Intellectual Functioning of Four-Year-Old Boys, *Developmental Psychology*, Vol. 6, 1972, p. 353.

3. Blancahard, R., and Biller, H., Father Availability and Academic Performance Among Third-Grade Boys, *Developmental Psychology*, Vol. 4, 1971, p. 301.

4. Sadker, M., and Sadker, D., Sexism in the Classroom, *Psychology Today*, March 1985, p. 54.

5. Purves, A., *Literature Education in Ten Countries*. New York: Wiley, 1973.

6. Fackelmann, K. "Flabby Teenage Years Presage Health Risks," *Science News*, Nov. 14, 1992, p. 326.

7. Martel, L., and Biller, H., *Stature and Stigma*. Lexington, MA: Lexington Books, 1987.

8. McCarthy, P., "Couch Potatoes Need Exercise," *Psychology Today*, August 1987, p. 13.

9. Eccles, J., Timmer, S., and O'Brien, K., *Time, Goods, and Well-Being*. Ann Arbor, MI: The Institute for Social Research, 1985.

10. Turning Youths to Science, *Washington Post*, January 23, 1989.

SUGGESTED READINGS

THE FAMILY FITNESS HANDBOOK by Glover, B. and Shepherd, J., Penguin, 1989.

THE PASSIONATE MIND: BRINGING UP A CREATIVE AND INTELLIGENT CHILD by Schulman, M., Free Press, 1991.

365 TV-FREE ACTIVITIES YOU CAN DO WITH YOUR CHILD by Bennett, S., and Bennett, R., Bob Adams, 1993.

Teens and Sexuality

Alex didn't like himself. Everyone else thought he was a successful, thirty-three-year-old lawyer and social worker. He thought he was a dismal failure. He lived alone but didn't want to be alone. He had lovers but couldn't fall in love or find a woman who satisfied him. He was full of doubts and fears and guilts, and he totally disapproved of himself. Alex lay the blame for his unhappiness at the feet of his family. From the moment Alex was born, he was the apple of his mother's eye. She constantly told him that he was a perfect prince, a unique and brilliant genius. At first, Alex enjoyed being the center of attraction and the object of his mother's worship. He tried to live up to her expectations by doing exactly what he was told, and when he got all A's in school, his mother called him "Einstein the second."

As Alex neared adolescence, he began to resent the way his mother treated him. Coming out of a restaurant, for instance, she would go on and on about what a good boy he had been. He had used his little napkin and his silverware, and he hadn't spilled any of his potatoes. A perfect little gentleman, his mother would say. "Fruit-cake, mother," Alex said to himself. "A little fruitcake is what you saw—and exactly what the training program was designed to produce."

Alex didn't want to be a fruitcake. His resentment soon turned into rebellion, and he quit being an obedient and helpless little boy. He began to fight with his parents. He wouldn't eat what he was supposed to eat. He wouldn't go to the synagogue. He took up a new hobby—masturbation. It was the only thing he had to himself, he said.

Masturbation wasn't the answer to Alex's problems. In fact, it only made matters worse. After years of doing only what he was supposed to do, he was now doing something he felt guilty about. He was in constant fear of getting caught, and he was terrified that he would give himself cancer. Even so, he continued to masturbate with a passion.

As an adult, Alex had similar problems. He had done everything his parents wanted him to do. He got straight A's in college, graduated at the top of his class, and was a respected member of the community who worked to solve other people's problems. But he couldn't solve his own problems. He wanted to be a competent and independent adult. He wanted to be a father and a husband, but his sexual desires made him go from woman to woman, from affair to affair, in search of yet another sexual conquest. He could not find a middle ground between what his parents wanted him to be, what his sexuality wanted him to be, and what he wanted himself to be.

Alex is Alex Portnoy, the confused hero of *Portnoy's Complaint*, Philip Roth's satiric novel about adolescence.[1] And like all good fiction, *Portnoy's Complaint* contains much that is true about human nature. Alex's search for himself is similar to what many adolescents go through trying to find an acceptable identity for themselves.

Alex was having what psychoanalyst Erik Erikson calls an identity crisis. According to Erikson, most adolescents go through an identity crisis as they try to find an acceptable identity for themselves. They have to stop being their parents' children and their teachers' students. They have to develop certain skills, talents, and social identities that will point them toward college or a career. They have to develop meaningful goals and values that will influence what they do for the rest of their lives. They have to explore their sexuality. Once they are able to pull all these things together in a firm and comfortable identity, they will be ready to deal successfully with other people and eventually to share life's intimacies with another person. Those who don't solve their identity crisis and who are unhappy with what they are may remain isolated from the closest forms of psychological sharing with others. In other words, if you don't love yourself, you can't love others.

Alex Portnoy didn't love himself because he didn't like the kind of person he had become, and he didn't like the fact that he couldn't settle down to a normal family and social life. He blamed his unhappiness on his family, and he may have been right to do so. Alex's father loved him, but he worked twelve hours a day and on weekends and didn't have a lot of time for his children. Alex's mother loved him, but she didn't give him room to grow into the kind of person he wanted to be. Alex's resulting rebelliousness led to constant family fights and turmoil, which further damaged his relationship with both parents.

As we have seen, a close relationship with one's parents, especially one's father, seems to be particularly important to the personal happiness and social development of both sons and daughters. Even benign neglect by a loving but distant or ineffective father can have lasting negative effects on personal development and social competence. Studies of young adults find that those who scored highest on measures of self-acceptance and personal and social adjustment had fathers who were nurturing and close to them. Those who scored lowest saw their fathers as having been negligent and rejecting.[2] And this carries over to the next generation. Parents who reported a high level of involvement with attentive and loving fathers tend to be socially and emotionally well adjusted and to have children who see them as being attentive and affectionate parents. The burden, of course, isn't entirely on fathers. Researchers find that the most well-adjusted men and women tend to be those who had closely involved fathers and mothers who were also closely involved with each other.[3]

Alex Portnoy's parents may have helped cause his identity crisis, but finding out who you are in the midst of raging hormones, raging parents, peer pressure, school pressure, and all the other pressures that come down on teenagers isn't easy. Many older children experience what Erikson calls "role confusion." They don't know exactly who they are or what they should be. Self-doubts, rebellion, and experimentation with different roles are often the result. But rebellion and confusion don't have to be part of growing up. In fact, the teenage years usually aren't half as bad as many parents expect them to be.

Psychological theories used to say that rebelliousness was a normal, even healthy, part of adolescence. Since the 1970s, however, more and more studies indicate that most teenagers and their parents actually feel close to each other and get along very well. Psychologist Anne C. Peterson and her colleagues, for example, monitored the lives of 335 young adolescents and found that the usual pattern of development is quite positive. More than half of those in the study seemed to be almost trouble-free, and approximately 30 percent had only intermittent problems. Only 15 percent exhibited the trouble and turmoil often associated with adolescence. Those with particularly positive and supportive parents showed the fewest negative effects.[4]

INTRODUCING YOUR CHILDREN TO THE SOCIAL WORLD

If you have been a close, loving father, you are likely to continue to have close relationships with your children as they go through adolescence. In fact, you've already gone a long way toward helping them to become independent and to develop realistic social and sexual identities. Your past and continued encouragement of their assertiveness, body pride, and basic self-esteem, for example, increases the likelihood that they will have successful social experiences with other teens and adults and easy, natural relationships with members of the other sex. And dealing with others is a vital part of a child's development at any age.

You, your wife, and the rest of your immediate family made up almost the entire social world of your infant.

But as that baby grew, so did his or her social life. Children begin to make close friends during the early school years, and this is important to their overall development and understanding of themselves. Other children let your children know such things as whether they are good-looking, likable, funny, or athletic. Other children give your children the opportunity to try out all the talents and values they have learned at home. As they grow older and begin to search for an identity, adolescents often join groups for support, which allows them to try out new ideas and fads on others who are also at the experimenting stage and are likely to be encouraging.

By the time they reach adolescence, your children will probably want to spend more time with their friends than they do with you. But this does not mean that your power as a father has diminished. Studies consistently show that throughout their lives children regard their parents' opinions more highly than they do those of their friends or other adults. Even during times of teenage rebellion, your children will still value your opinions, assuming that you have had an ongoing, meaningful relationship. And your job is to sustain that relationship while encouraging your child's social development, independence, and competence.

As a loving and nurturing father, you will play an especially important role in helping your children develop the capacity to build meaningful relationships with others. Psychologist Ross Parke and his colleagues have found that the way fathers play with their young sons and daughters influences the quality of their children's relationships with other boys and girls. The father's ability to be responsive to his children's initiative during play is especially important. If the father is excessively controlling or domineering, he does not give his children the opportunity to learn effective social skills. As a consequence, they may be rejected or neglected by other children,[5] a situation that can carry over to the teenage and adult years.

For a child, however, the father–mother relationship is usually the most significant example of social behavior. How you show your affection for your wife—whether you are aloof or loving, formal or relaxed—is closely watched and imitated by your children in their own relationships. If you and your wife are considerate of each other's feelings and needs, it is likely that your children will develop positive attitudes toward both males and females and will demonstrate respect for the rights of others.

How you treat your other children is equally important in their social development because one of the first really close relationships a child is apt to have is with a brother or sister. If that relationship is close and affectionate, it sets the tone for the quality of later friendships and love relationships. If you are a loving father and are able to share your time with all of your children, they will follow your example and learn to treat each other and their friends equally, respectfully, and affectionately. If you favor one child or if you are aloof and distant, your children will have to fight for your attention, which can exacerbate sibling rivalry and affect how your children learn to deal with others.

Your dealings outside the family also affect your children's social development. In your work and play, you have contact with other men and women of many social levels. What your children learn from how you behave in different social settings will be an important element in their social development.

To guide your children through the teen years with a minimum of stress and trouble, you can do the following:

- Don't have your own identity crisis just because you have a teenager in the house and expect the worst. Some men aren't sure whether they are supposed to be a friend or a disciplinarian. Some do things like insisting that their children call them by their first name and even avoiding disciplining their children. Others go too far in the other direction, feeling that they have to maintain a certain amount of distance in order to be effective fathers. If you have been the kind of father described in this book, you should have little problem with such an identity crisis. You will feel comfortable being friends with your adolescent as well as being a realistic limit setter because both roles stem from your sense of effectiveness as a father.

- Remember that adolescents are developing their independence and a mind of their own, a mind that may not always agree with yours. Don't expect the worst, but be prepared for conflict, usually in the form of nagging, squabbling, and bickering, which is more common during adolescence than at any other time, except, perhaps, during the terrible twos. The worst time is usually between the ages of ten and thirteen, and it typically ends by fifteen or sixteen, depending on whether puberty comes early or late.[6] Arguments with teenagers can be stressful, but they usually do not undo a close father-child bond. If the conflict becomes physically or psychologically abusive, however, you should seek professional help.

- Remember that your young adolescents may be going through a tough time. Their bodies and brains are changing rapidly, and they are beginning to look, behave, and think differently. They are also beginning to be treated differently: Parents, teachers, and other adults expect more of them. They may be switching to a new school, and facing new responsibilities with a new set of people to deal with. All of this can be quite stressful, and your youngsters will need all the support, encouragement, and understanding you can provide.

- As your children grow older, encourage their continued social development by letting them learn from how you deal with a wide range of people—your boss, your co-workers, the people who work for you. Introduce them to different aspects of society and let them see what your social world is like. Contact with different kinds of people can be especially important in preventing racial or religious prejudice in your children.

- Let your children get to know your friends. When friends visit, don't just send your kids off to play by themselves. Children don't have to be the center of attention, but they shouldn't be excluded from adult gatherings, especially those that involve men, with whom your children may not have had much contact.

- Spend individual time with your children and try not to be jealous of their friends, which is often the case with men who haven't spent much time at home with their children. As your children grow older, you will have to share them more and more with their friends.

- Get to know your children's friends—not to keep tabs on them but to show them that you are interested in their social life. If you know their friends, you can also explain what kinds of people you think they should avoid. You can't realistically forbid a teenager to see certain people, but you can explain why you don't like the way some of them behave. If your explanation is presented calmly and rationally—"Carol bothers me because she doesn't seem to have any respect for other people's feelings"—your teenager may even agree.

You can meet and get to know your children's friends

by including one or more of them when you take your children to a movie, a ball game, ice skating—whatever you and they can enjoy doing together. This gives you a chance to see how your children get along with others and gives them a chance to see you in action. If you are considerate of their friends, they will learn how much you value being considerate. If your children also get to spend time with the fathers of their friends, they will get a chance to compare the social styles of different types of men.

- Encourage assertiveness and independence and help your children develop their social lives, but remember that they are all different. Not all teenagers want to join groups or teams or go to dances. Some are quite shy, whereas others are extroverted and eager to meet new people. Accept the individuality of each of your children and don't force them into social situations where they may feel uncomfortable.

INTRODUCING YOUR CHILDREN TO THE SEXUAL WORLD

Young Portnoy had a problem with sex. He felt socially inadequate and sexually inhibited. As a teenager, he could barely bring himself to talk to a girl. But even if there were no such thing as sexual inhibition, people would still have difficulties relating to the other sex because sexual problems often stem from interpersonal, or social, problems. A boy who is shy with girls or a girl who is shy with boys is not necessarily sexually inhibited. He or she may simply lack the ability to deal with others, male or female, on a person-to-person level. Your son's or daughter's relationship with the other sex is a special kind of social relationship that depends to a large extent on their overall social abilities. And just as you affect the social development of your children, you will have a major impact on their sexual development. If you and your wife have provided your sons and daughters with a strong sense of self-esteem, assertiveness, nurturance, and pride in their sex roles, they are very likely to develop healthy relationships with the other sex.

Your son's relationship with girls, for instance, will be based on the quality of his masculinity, which you have influenced by the example you set with your wife and with other women: Your son will watch how you treat his sisters, other girls his age, your wife, her friends, and your own female friends and associates. If you treat women with respect as fellow humans and not as some stereotyped category called "female," your son will be encouraged to do the same.

Your son will also learn from observing how you react to the sexual attractiveness of women. When you say something nice about a beautiful woman walking down the street or an attractive anchorwoman on television, you show your son that you value your sexuality as a natural part of life rather than as something to be hidden or something that children shouldn't know about. Boys who do not have a strong relationship with their fathers or who suffer from father absence or neglect may not learn such things and may have problems relating to girls and women. Without a solid gender identity, they are less likely to feel secure with females. As they mature, they may lack confidence in asserting their romantic intentions or may go to the other extreme by behaving like a Don Juan, desperately trying to make themselves feel masculine by attempting to add continually to their list of sexual conquests. Naturally, this interferes with healthy sexual relationships and the development of a successful marriage.

Fathers are equally important in their daughter's sexual development. You are the first man in her life, and she will see you as a model for all men. During the first years of her life, she will begin to realize that she is a girl and that you are a man. As she grows, she will look to you for a reaction to her feminine development. And as she enters adolescence, your role as a male model and as a judge of her femininity will become even more important. If you have a good relationship with her, she will be able to turn to you as well as to her mother for help in weathering the emotional storms of her relationships with boys. With your affection, understanding, encouragement, and protection, she will be prepared to enter into meaningful relationships with men. Researchers have found, for example, that college-age women who have long-term romantic relationships have had closer relationships with their fathers than have women who are not romantically involved. On the other hand, women who have unstable sexual relationships and broken marriages are more likely to have had poor relationships with their fathers.

The importance of fathers to the sexuality of their daughters can be seen quite clearly in a study conducted by psychologist Mavis Hetherington and her colleagues.[7] They compared three groups of teenage girls who had grown up either with or without fathers. One group had lost their fathers because of divorce and had no contact with their fathers since the divorce. The second group had been reared by widowed mothers, and the third group came from families with both a mother and father. Few of these young women had any noticeable behavior problems and all were doing reasonably well in school, but there were definite differences in the way they reacted to men.

As part of the study, each girl was shown into an

office where she was interviewed by a man. There were three chairs in the office for the girls to choose from, and the daughters of divorce usually chose the chair closest to the man and sat in an open-legged sprawling posture. They leaned forward toward the man, looked into his eyes, smiled often, and were talkative, forward, and flirtatious. Girls whose fathers had died acted quite differently. They sat stiffly upright in the chair farthest from the man, tended to turn their shoulders away from him, kept their legs together, and did not smile, make eye contact, or talk as much as the other girls did. In general, they were extremely shy and timid with the man. Girls from a two-parent home acted in a manner between these extremes and were much more at ease with the man than were girls from the father-absent groups, who tended to pluck at their clothes, pull at their fingers, and twirl their hair. The differences among the girls did not show up when they were interviewed by a woman.

The researchers found that the attitudes displayed by the girls during the interviews were also apparent in their other relationships with males. Girls from divorced families sought more attention and praise from men than did girls in the other two groups. They were more likely to spend much of their time in places where young men could be found—gymnasiums, carpentry and machine shops—and tended to stay near the boys at community and school dances. In their search for attention, these girls tended to use their bodies. They dated more often and tended to have sex more often and at an earlier age than girls of the other two groups. Girls whose fathers had died tended to avoid males. They started dating much later than the others and seemed to be sexually inhibited. At one of the dances attended by the psychologists, these girls avoided the areas where the boys gathered and two of them even hid in the bathroom for the entire evening.

These findings suggest that when a father is not part of the family, this has a big influence on a girl's attitude toward men. Interviews with the girls indicated that the daughters of divorced parents tended to dislike their fathers, perhaps because of the mothers' negative attitude toward their ex-husbands and because the girls felt that their fathers had abandoned them. Girls whose fathers had died were more likely to remember their fathers as idealized images or models of masculinity that no other man could live up to. Although they expressed it differently, both groups of father-absent girls were insecure in their dealings with men. And insecurity in relating to men was greatest in the girls who lost their fathers before the age of five.

The researchers continued to monitor the development of these girls for several years and found that the effects of father absence last long past the teenage years. The daughters from divorced families seemed to have especially troubled relationships with men. They tended to marry at an earlier age and to be pregnant at the time of marriage. Many of their marriages ended in separation or divorce, and interviews indicated that they had married less adequate men than did those in the other groups. The men they married had lower educational and vocational accomplishments and many had been in trouble with the law. In contrast, the daughters of widows tended to marry successful and ambitious men who were overly inhibited in their social interactions. The women from intact families made the most realistic and successful choices of husbands and reported more sexual satisfaction (including number of orgasms) in their marriages than did women who grew up without fathers.

How can you help your children get the right messages about sexuality and relationships?

- Remember that how you handle your half of the husband-wife sexual relationship can be your children's most important model of healthy male behavior. They will watch closely and may imitate your behavior and attitudes in their own relationships.
- Remember that your attitudes toward sex are communicated to your children long before they reach adolescence or even school age. What would happen, for instance, if one of your children walked in while you and your wife were making love? Would you be ashamed or harsh with the child or merely annoyed but accepting? Your attitude will be remembered for a long time.
- Take an active role in the formation of your children's attitudes about sex. It is important that both parents communicate healthy attitudes toward sexuality, but you may be in a better position than your wife to foster openness about sex to your children. As a boy you were probably exposed to fewer inhibitions about sex than your wife was. You were probably never cautioned about being "taken advantage of" or told you were in danger of getting a bad reputation for being "that kind of boy."
- You may have to overcome both your own and society's attitudes about male sexual exploits as "conquests." If you can see sex as a natural part of life, as a special social relationship between a man and a woman, you will probably be able to give your children a healthy attitude about sex.
- Prepare your children well in advance for the time when they will become sexually active. Have frank and open discussions with them about contraception and

safe sex. Don't give them the impression that sex is dirty or dangerous, but make sure they are aware of the possibilities of pregnancy, AIDS, and other sexually transmitted diseases.

- Share your values and opinions on sexuality with your children, but remember that sexuality involves far more than physical interaction between two people. Stress the importance of love, concern, and responsibility in any sexual relationship. Explain the reasons for your approach to appropriate sexual behavior, whether they are religious standards or based more on individual conscience.

- Do not pressure your adolescents to conform to your attitudes, but rather consistently express views that indicate a respect for the other sex. Your example is the best way to increase the likelihood that they will eventually adopt similar values.

- Don't expect to know everything that is going on in your adolescent children's sex lives. Even if you have had a close relationship with them, they may not want to talk about their sex lives with you. Older children and adolescents need to feel independent from their parents, especially on issues of intimacy and sexuality. Constructive fathering means being a concerned and loving advisor, not a controller of your child's personal decisions. Your high expectations will be much more effective in the long run than ultimatums or intimidation. Accept the fact that your maturing children need to take responsibility for their own relationships.

- Remember that you can't supervise a teenager twenty-four hours a day. Many fathers virtually lock up their teenage children, especially their daughters, in an attempt to keep them from becoming sexually active. This, however, is not likely to foster close family relations. Set reasonable times for teenagers to be

home at night, and make it clear that you will be there
if they need your help.

- If there are indications your teenager is involved in a
harmful relationship, try to be a concerned advisor
rather than an authoritarian father. If, for example, a
seventeen-year-old daughter has been dating a young
man who is insensitive and irresponsible, try to be
supportive and help her to end the relationship without
issuing any ultimatums. As most fathers of teenagers
discover sooner or later, attempts to control their children's behavior are doomed to failure. But if you have
a close relationship, it is highly likely that your values
will influence your children's behavior.

- Remember that your relationship with your daughter
will be especially important to her social and sexual
adjustment. If she doesn't learn to trust you, she may
have difficulty trusting other men and forming healthy
sexual relationships. Boys who have inadequate or distant fathers usually have plenty of opportunities to
form relationships with females—mothers, teachers,
baby-sitters. Girls who have inadequate fathers are
much less likely to encounter a man who will be consistently kind and sensitive toward them.

- Coach your daughter on how to relate to males. For
instance, you can tell her what makes a girl attractive
to boys in more than a physical sense. you can encourage her to be assertive and emphasize that women are
not passive creatures to be manipulated by men.

- Do not discuss sexuality simply in terms of the dangers
of being manipulated or hurt by a partner. Scare tac-
tics don't lead to healthy sexual or social development.
A major goal with both sons and daughters should be
to diffuse potential fear and mistrust of the other sex.
The best way to do this is by teaching them about sex.

HELPING YOUR CHILDREN UNDERSTAND THEIR SEXUALITY

Unfortunately, many parents avoid teaching their children about sex. Some never received any sex education as children and repeat the cycle of silence from generation to generation. Others are simply embarrassed, and some continue to believe that telling children about sex will make them want to have sex. But numerous studies have shown that sex education actually lowers rates of sexual activity among teenagers. Those who have had sex education, either at home or in school, are less likely than adolescents of the same age to have had sex. Those who received sex education at home as well as at school are the least likely to be sexually active.[8] Parental resistance to sex education because it may lead to early sexual activity is eroding, however, in the face of the AIDS epidemic. More than 60 percent of parents now report that they talk to their children about sex—twice as many as in 1985.[9]

It is ignorance and unresolved curiosity, not knowledge, that are harmful says sex educator Sol Gordon of the Institute for Family Research and Education at Syracuse University.[10] "Our failure to tell children what they want and need to know," he says, "is one reason we have the highest rates of out-of-wedlock teen pregnancy and abortion of any highly developed country in the world."

What do adolescents want and need to know about sex? Gordon and his colleagues have received more than 50,000 questions from teenagers across the country. They don't want to know about fallopian tubes, he says. They want to know about homosexuality, penis size, masturbation, female orgasm, oral and anal sex, and the answer to such questions as, How can I tell if I'm really in love? What is sexual desire? What is the best contraceptive? When is a girl most likely to get pregnant? One of the most frequently asked questions is, Why are boys only interested in girls for sex?

The time to start sex education is during infancy. Babies are naturally curious about all parts of their bodies, and they should not be kept from exploring them. To start off by punishing children for their curiosity is a mistake. To tell young children silly stories about the stork or the cabbage patch is also a mistake. If you answer their questions truthfully and honestly and at their level of interest and understanding, it will be much easier for you to discuss sexual matters when they are adolescents and are especially in need of information. If you have not laid the groundwork for sex education early, you may find it difficult to cope with adolescent sexuality. If you have had an honest, open relationship with your children, you should have little trouble relating to them at this time. They should have a clear idea by now of what your feelings are about sexual relationships. Because there is a good chance that their first sexual encounter will occur before marriage, probably during the high school years, they should know your feelings on premarital sex. They should also have confidence that despite your opinions, you recognize that they have the right to control their own lives and that you are only a concerned, loving advisor. Your high expectations of them will have more effect on their behavior than any threat or reprimand could have.

Fathers have traditionally been the sex educators of their sons; mothers, of their daughters. But both you and your wife should be involved in the sex education of both your sons and daughters. There are unique roles in sex education that only a father can assume with a daughter and a mother, with a son. Yet, because you have experienced many of the same feelings and had the same kind of physical development as your son, you can be particularly helpful in telling him what to expect as a growing man. If you have a close relationship with him, what you tell him will carry more weight than what he hears from his friends or even what he learns in school. You can explain to him and assure him that spontaneous erections and wet dreams are normal. You can assure him that his penis is normal. Young boys can be quite overawed by the size of their father's genitals, and you can help his confidence by letting him know that he will also develop normally.

You can assure him that masturbation is perfectly natural and harmless and that almost all men do it. You might even joke about it with him (as he surely does with his friends) and let him know that masturbation is not dangerous or shameful. Surveys indicate that more than 90 percent of men and more than 60 percent of women masturbate at some time in their lives, though men do it about twice as often as women. And about twice as many boys as girls have masturbated by the age of thirteen.

When your son asks about the differences between male and female genitals, explain it in positive rather than negative terms. Say women have their sexual organs inside, not that they "don't have a penis." Don't start him off with the attitude that males are superior because they have something women don't have. Your emphasis on genital equality, along with your treatment of women as equals, will impress on your son that women are to be valued as persons as well as sex partners.

Besides the details about human anatomy, you can help your son in his social relationships with girls. When he bombs out with a girl, assure him that it doesn't mean that he is inferior or unattractive. When he makes a big hit with a girl, help him see his success as the start of a personal, equal relationship, not a conquest.

Your daughter's sex education may be much more difficult than your son's for several reasons. First, there is the traditional male shyness about discussing sex with females. There may also be a subtle fear of being sexually aroused by your daughter while discussing sex. But just as your wife can talk about women with your son with a special kind of expertise, you can talk about men with your daughter. You can allay myths and fears about boys that often circulate among girls and can answer your daughter's questions about male anatomy.

You can be a particularly good coach for your daughter on how to relate to boys. You can emphasize that sexual intimacy, although extremely important, is only one part of male–female relationships, and you can be an example of a man who values his sexuality but does not allow it to obscure other dimensions of his personality.

There are many other ways you can help your children be secure—and responsible—in their sexuality:

- Do not be embarrassed to talk about sex with your children. You have to overcome such feelings if your children are to be comfortable in their sexuality. Some fathers avoid introducing sex education to their kids altogether, but even this is actually a kind of negative sex education. By not mentioning sex, you are telling your children that it is not a fit subject to discuss.
- Don't scold or punish your children for simply being curious or wanting to know about sexual issues. Make it very clear that they can come to you with questions and concerns about any kind of social or sexual situation. When they ask questions about sex, give direct and honest responses, and begin to build a healthy

foundation for more detailed discussions as they grow older.

- Don't lecture your children and turn them into passive listeners. Let them ask the questions. If there are topics that they don't know enough about to bring up or are reluctant to discuss, try to introduce the subject subtly at an appropriate time. If, for example, your child shows interest in a love scene from a movie, you could say "It looks like they're going to make love." Then leave it open for the child to ask questions or make comments. The more quality, one-on-one time you spend with your children, the more likely there are to be natural opportunities for discussing important topics.

- Tell your children about homosexuality and tell them it is not all right to be antigay. It is just as wrong to be antigay as it is to be racist or sexist.

- Remember that teaching your children about sex also involves teaching them about love. Many fathers think all their children want to know is what goes where. Tell your children that love can be expressed through sexuality but that being responsible and considerate of another person's feelings is equally important.

- If you don't know everything you think you should know about sex, get a good book and do some research. You might learn something new, and you will be prepared to answer your children's questions accurately.

- If you are shy about sex education or don't think you are a good teacher, buy some sex education books written for children. Let them read the books and invite them to ask questions. This is a good way to break the ice. Read *Portnoy's Complaint*. It will help you remember what it was like to be a constantly horny teenager. Read Anne Frank's *Diary of a Young Girl* to eavesdrop on some of the thoughts of a young girl having her first period, feeling her breasts grow, falling in love. Encourage your teenagers to read good books about adolescence. It will help them realize that they aren't the only ones going through what they are going through, and it will help you and them bring up topics that might be difficult to discuss.

- In dealing with sexual matters with a son or daughter, one of your aims should be to head off an irrational fear of the other sex, including potential anxieties about injury to the genitals. You should tell your children about pregnancy and sexually transmitted diseases, but do not cite these dangers as reasons for not having sex. Instead, explain the danger of pregnancy in terms of responsibility—adolescents aren't prepared to be responsible for a child. Explain AIDS and sexually transmitted diseases the way you would any other disease, emphasizing how to avoid them and making it clear that the disease has nothing to do with the morality of sex, that morality comes from the conscience, not from a virus or germ.
- Stress the advantages of waiting to engage in a full-fledged sexual relationship until there is a clear and mature commitment. Because your children may not follow this advice, make sure that they are fully informed about contraceptive methods.

DEALING WITH TEENAGE TURMOIL

Portnoy, like many teenagers, simply aggravated his parents. Unfortunately, some teenagers do much more. The worst carry guns to school, get into fights with rival gang members, steal cars, get pregnant, get high on drugs, get thrown in jail. They develop antisocial personalities and become so-called juvenile delinquents. Why? There are many reasons, ranging from poverty and racism to psychological and learning disorders, but many troubled teenagers—whether from the inner city or the affluent suburbs—did not have adequate fathers. Researchers used to believe that mothers shape and are largely responsible for their children's personalities and thus their problems. Today, however, we have consistent evidence that poor fathering is often a major factor, particularly for behavior disorders and delinquency. Studies of delinquents find that most of them had very little attention or guidance from their fathers. Compared with fathers of other children, those of delinquents typically give little direction and share fewer plans, activities, and interests with their children. This pattern of neglect is often accompanied by verbal abuse and ridicule, which can destroy a child's self-esteem.

When children feel that their fathers don't value them, they sometimes begin to feel that they are worthless and that no one really cares about them. Whether or not they become antisocial or delinquent, the extreme behaviors of many adolescents are often a desperate attempt to get their fathers to pay attention to them. To some extent, a caring mother can act as a buffer against father neglect, but one caring adult simply cannot give as much attention and guidance as two involved parents. When a basically adequate mother has all the responsibility for rearing children, whether in a one- or two-parent family, she is likely to feel overwhelmed in her attempts to set limits and control her adolescent children. There are certainly inadequate mothers who contribute to their children's delinquent behavior, but the lack of an adequate father is far more common among troubled teens.

Delinquent girls are likely to have had fathers who were cold, rejecting, and hostile toward them. Frustrated with her father's behavior, a daughter may run away from home or get involved in a sexual relationship that she hopes will free her from an abusive father. Delinquency in boys is more often associated with violence and physical aggressiveness. Psychologist David Lisak has also found that poor fathering can be linked with sexual aggressiveness in young men. Studies of rapists conducted in the 1950s and 1960s often put the blame on mothers, who were accused of dominating, rejecting, nagging, seducing, or being intrusive and ungiving to sons who later raped women. When these studies were conducted, says Lisak, the only people interested in studying rapists were psychoanalysts, and they had a ready-made theory to fall back on. Following Freud, they concluded that the rapist is angry at his mother. He can't attack her, so he takes out his anger on other women through the act of rape. Curiously, the men in these studies had not been asked about their fathers. So Lisak conducted his own study of rapists and found that the men who had the worst relationships with their fathers also had the most hostility toward women, the greatest need to dominate and control women, and the most rigid beliefs in sexual stereotypes.

How does this happen? Lisak says it is the father's job to demonstrate and help his sons become appropriately masculine. If the father fails by being distant or by not providing the kind of relationship that shows his sons how to be appropriately masculine, they may not develop a secure masculine identity. Realizing this, they search for ways to reinforce their masculinity. They join gangs or fraternities, for example, that support their insecure gender identity. The rapists Lisak studied were college men, and almost all of them were part of formal or informal all-male groups that had as their primary activity the exaltation of hypermasculine values and the denigration of women. And in study after study, Lisak says, sexually aggressive men have been found to score higher than nonaggressive men on measures of hypermasculinity, sex-role-stereotyped beliefs and attitudes, hostility toward women, and the need to dominate and control women. This combination of traits, Lisak believes, describes men disposed to commit rape.[11]

Parents often blame their children's rebelliousness and antisocial behavior on their children's friends, and this can be the case. But it is also the case that teenagers who feel neglected at home often turn to other teens to fill the vacuum in their lives. In many cases, they show poor judgment in choosing friends because of a desperate need for acceptance. Seeking acceptance, they succumb to peer pressure and are likely to go along with whatever the other teens are up to—drinking, drug abuse, and the kind of behavior that gets them in trouble.

Fathers, of course, can't be blamed for everything troubled teens do. The incidence of emotional disturbance is higher among children who had absent or inadequate fathers, but there are many psychologically healthy and effective fathers who have troubled children. These children may have a genetic or biological disorder or some other problem that has nothing to do with their father. But even if a father did not contribute to his children's problems, he has a responsibility to help solve them. When parents work together to help a troubled child, there is a much better chance that the family will be able to cope with the problem. Unfortunately, many fathers avoid this responsibility and revert to form, allowing the child to become the mother's responsibility.

To encourage healthy attitudes and behavior toward others, you can do the following:

- Remember that teenagers cannot be expected to treat themselves and others with respect if you do not value them as individuals. If you are hostile, restrictive, or neglectful, you may be driving your children away from you and undermining their mental health.
- If you have a troubled teenager, face the possibility that your behavior may be at least in part to blame and try to be even more nurturing and involved than you may have been.
- Listen closely to your teenagers and try to understand their problems rather than ridicule or punish them for their shortcomings.
- Make sure that punishment and discipline are not the only ways you have of interacting with your children. They may need a lot of guidance, but they also need your respect and loving attention.
- Make sure that you set a consistently good example for your children. Do not tell them not to do things that you do. Don't, for example, smoke or drink and expect them not to do the same. Don't physically abuse your children and expect them not to be aggressive. Don't be derogatory toward them and expect them to be sensitive to others.
- Avoid fights and arguments with your wife. Parents who constantly criticize and demean each other undermine their children's emotional security and are poor models of intimacy to their children.
- Seek professional help if you have a child with an emotional, learning, or behavioral problem. In many cases, it may be necessary to seek family therapy, because the child's problem will probably affect the entire family. Even if your child's problems don't stem from your behavior, remember that your negative reaction to them can make matters worse. On the other hand,

your involvement in treatment can do much to improve the situation.

REFERENCES

1. Roth, P., *Portnoy's Complaint*. New York: Random House, 1967.

2. Reuter, M., and Biller, H., Perceived Paternal Nurturance-Availability in Personality Adjustment Among College Males, *Journal of Consulting and Clinical Psychology*, Vol. 40, 1973, p. 339.

3. Biller, H., *Fathers and Families: Paternal Factors in Child Development*. Westport, CT: Auburn House, 1993.

4. Petersen, A., Those Gangly Years, *Psychology Today*, September 1987, p. 28.

5. Parke, R., et al., in R. Peters and R. McMahan (Eds.), *Marriages and Families: Behavioral Treatments and Processes*. New York: Brunner/Mazel, 1988.

6. Steinberg, L., Bound to Bicker, *Psychology Today*, September 1987, p. 36.

7. Hetherington, M., "Effects of Father-Absence on Personality Development in Adolescent Daughters," *Developmental Psychology*, Vol. 7, 1972, p. 313.

8. Bozzi, V., "Sex: Education and Experience," *Psychology Today*, June 1986, p. 10.

9. "Talking About Sex . . . Parent to Child," Planned Parenthood survey results, *Psychology Today*, March 1989, p. 18.

10. Gordon, S., What Kids Need to Know, *Psychology Today*, October 1986, p. 22.

11. Lisak, D., "The Gender System, the Father-Son Relationship and Sexual Aggression" paper presented at the meeting of the American Psychological Association, Washington, DC, 1992.

SUGGESTED READINGS

YOUR TEN TO FOURTEEN YEAR OLD by Ames, L., Ilg, F., and Baker, S., Delacorte, 1989.

ALL GROWN UP AND NO PLACE TO GO: TEENAGERS IN CRISIS by Elkind, D., Addison-Wesley, 1984.

THE PROCESS OF PARENTING by Brooks, G., Mayfield, 1991.

FATHER HUNGER: FATHERS, DAUGHTERS AND FOOD by Maine, M., Gurze Books, 1991.

PARENTING TEENAGERS: SYSTEMATIC TRAINING FOR EFFECTIVE PARENTING OF TEENS by Dinkmeyer, D., and McKay, G., American Guidance Service, 1990.

9

Single, Part-Time, Step-, and Other Fathers

Dennis is a special kind of guy, part of a relatively new but growing phenomenon. He is a single father in a society that has traditionally awarded custody of children of divorce to the mother. Dennis fought for and won custody of his two children, and now he is learning what single mothers have known for a long time—that raising a family while trying to earn a living is not an easy job. He realizes that parenting works best as a two-person endeavor and that his situation will require special dedication and effort. Dennis is learning how to use the washer and dryer, pack lunches, talk to teachers, and do all the things his wife used to do for him and the kids. Through all of this, Dennis is also learning something even more important—that he can truly nurture his children and derive a great deal of satisfaction from helping them grow into successful adults.

There is a lot to learn from men like Dennis, social work researcher. Geoffrey Grief, for example, found that one of the toughest struggles single fathers have is balancing their work and family commitments. Many have to curtail their job responsibilities, avoid overtime, change jobs, and sometimes face quitting or being fired. "The father who formerly defined himself as a worker first and a father second must shift his values, accept less income, change his view of himself as a worker and try to adapt to conflicting demands," explains Grief.[1]

Another problem single fathers face is finding time to develop a social life while rearing children. And they find it especially difficult to develop successful love relationships. Most of the people who divorce, for example, do remarry, but half of those marriages also fail. And one of the primary reasons they fail, says Grief, "is because of problems of dealing with the children from the first marriage. The father may be caught in the middle between his children and the new spouse or lover, whom the children may not respect. Many of these fathers will be forced to side with their children, and the relationships then fail."

How do single fathers fare as fathers? Most research indicates that single fathers approach the job much the way single mothers do. A study that compared single fathers with single mothers found no significant differences between them regarding their understanding of the physical, emotional, and social aspects of parenting.

Fathers and mothers provided about the same amount of hugs, well-balanced meals, and piano lessons.

Even though men and women may approach single parenthood similarly and though there is no evidence that mothers are better than fathers at rearing children, there are differences in the way they affect their children. Psychologists John Santrock and Richard Warshuk examined the effects of custody on boys and girls between the ages of six and eleven and found that boys generally do better with their fathers, and girls, with their mothers.[2] The same-sex parent and child are more likely to have a sense of mutual understanding and common interests. Single parents usually find it easier to communicate with children of the same sex and have fewer discipline problems with them. However, the researchers found that it is the single father's or mother's relative ability to communicate and provide structure and security for the child over and above the parent's gender that is the most important factor in the family's adjustment.

These and numerous other studies all indicate that despite some difficulties single fathers can meet the challenges of parenthood. And if the divorce rate stays as high as it is and the divorce courts continue to give fathers a greater share in the lives of their children, more men like Dennis may learn that they can rear children as well as women can.

Here are some things you can do to give your children the best chance possible for a fulfilling future:

- If you are a single father and your children's mother is available and willing, encourage her involvement in child rearing as much as possible. Even if you are

Superdad, two parents are almost always better than one.

- No matter how busy you are taking care of the practical side of being a single father, make sure that you spend some special time with your children every day. It is important, especially for young children, to have the predictable presence of at least one parent for two or more hours of quality time every day. Do not, however, feel that you have to spend twice as much time with a child to make up for the absence of a mother. Twice as much time does not necessarily produce twice as good a relationship.

- Don't get so involved in being a father that you don't have any quality time for yourself. You need some time away from your children as well as time together. If you sacrifice all of your own interests trying to be two parents, the inevitable frustrations can lead to resentment and interfere with your father–child relationship. If your children are as adorable as you probably think they are, you shouldn't have much trouble getting someone to watch them once in a while.

CHILDREN OF DIVORCE

Single fathers, like Dennis, are the exception, but divorce is not. More than a million couples in this country get divorced every year, and two-thirds of them have children. These children of divorce are a rapidly growing population and one of the most thoroughly studied in this country. What most studies show is that divorce can be harmful to everyone involved. In some cases, divorce is less harmful to the children than living with battling parents. But in almost every case, divorce brings with it stress, conflict, and trauma for the parents and for the children, with the children being most likely to suffer from inadequate fathering because most of them end up living with their mothers all or most of the time.

One of the most important studies of the effects of divorce on children was conducted by psychologist Judith Wallerstein and her colleagues, who did extensive interviews with family members just after the separation and one, five, ten, and fifteen years later.[3] The first thing they found was that children, no matter what their age or family circumstances, do not respond well to divorce. Without exception, all of the children indicated a desire for their parents to stay together. Even after the divorce, most fantasized that their parents would remarry. There were, however, differences in the way children of different ages reacted, with the youngest children being the most affected.

Two- and three-year-olds were particularly likely to regress, to become more babylike. They appeared to be bewildered and angry and would cling to any adult. This type of regression was brief if the children received a good deal of loving attention from adult family members, but children whose mothers were devastated by the divorce appeared very depressed and developmentally delayed even a year after the divorce. Poor self-image and loss of self-esteem were seen among the three- and four-year-olds, who seemed to feel responsible for their parents' divorce. Most of the five- and six-year-olds weathered the divorce without showing obvious signs of distress, which suggests, as much other research does, that children are particularly vulnerable to father loss before the age of five.

Many of the seven- and eight-year-olds seemed intensely sad in response to the divorce, especially about not having as much contact with their fathers. They appeared to be quite frightened about the consequences of the divorce and all seemed desperately to want their parents back together again. The relatively mature nine- and ten-year-olds were able to deal with the separation more realistically, but loneliness, physical symptoms, feelings of shame, and an intense anger toward the parents were quite common. About half of these children seemed to be coping adequately a year after the divorce, but they still had feelings of sadness and bitterness. The other half in this age group were severely handicapped by feelings of low self-esteem and depression and had difficulties with other children and in school.

For adolescents, the divorce meant pain, anger, sadness, and resentment when their parents began to date. Those who were relatively mature at the time of the divorce and were able to maintain some distance from their parents' conflicts seemed to be doing better by the end of the first year after the divorce. Those who had emotional and social problems before the divorce tended to have even more serious difficulties afterward.

Five years later, most of these children were still showing signs of distress. About one-third of them had rather severe personal and social problems. They had particularly strong feelings of loneliness, alienation, and depression and were extremely dissatisfied with their lives. Another group had a mixed reaction, showing typical ups and downs with some evidence that the divorce still had negative effects on their self-esteem and overall competence. Only one-third of the children survived the divorce relatively unscathed and were doing well personally, socially, and educationally. Many factors were involved in the way these children adjusted to divorce, but a crucial factor was the continuing close involvement of the father, which was associated with healthy adjustment for both boys and girls.

Ten and fifteen years after the divorce, more than half of the children were still having difficulties. Those who were youngest at the time of the divorce, however, seemed to be adjusting more successfully than the older children, at least with respect to dealing with memories of family conflict and being relatively optimistic about their own futures. The eleven- to seventeen-year-olds, for example, were not as preoccupied with troubled memories of family life as were the nineteen- to twenty-eight-year-olds, many of whom were now having serious difficulties in their attempts to establish meaningful love relationships and career commitments.

The children in this study were not compared with similar children from intact families, so it cannot be said for certain that divorce was the only factor that led to their many troubles. Still, information collected from these children of divorce during the fifteen years of the study clearly point to divorce, along with father absence or father neglect, as the overriding factors in their often troubled lives.

Unfortunately, divorce is a reality in the lives of many children. But father absence does not have to be. The absolute importance of fathers in the lives of their children has been clearly demonstrated, and the courts and society are beginning to expect fathers to be more responsible parents. In a fully equal world, divorced fathers and mothers would share in all aspects of their children's lives. Until this is the reality, divorced fathers should do everything reasonably possible to stay closely involved with their children. If divorce is a factor in the lives of you and your children, you should try to make sure that it does as little harm as possible. Even after you and your wife are divorced, you both have a lasting responsibility to your children, and there are many ways you can help your children cope with divorce.

- When you first begin to think about divorce, make sure you consider carefully the long-term effects it is likely to have on the lives of your children. As Wallerstein's and many other studies show, they can be quite devastating. Don't rush into a quick separation or divorce. Take time to consider the possibility of a reconciliation. If that is not possible, at least take time to prepare your family for what is likely to be a stressful situation. Explain to your children that you and your wife really tried to work out your problems but just couldn't do it. Make sure they understand that the decision to divorce was between you and your wife and is not their responsibility.

- As soon as you know that divorce is inevitable, tell your children what to expect in a divorce and help them get ready for the changes in your lives. Work out a shared parenting arrangement before the divorce, and establish regular times to be with your children as a way of helping them get used to the new situation. Seek professional help if you and your wife cannot work out cooperative arrangements for child care.

- Work especially hard to be a close and concerned father immediately after the divorce. Your children will be particularly in need of your help at this time. The divorce may be as stressful on you as it is on your children, and your own psychological problems may interfere with your ability to be the best of fathers. It may even take you two or more years to get back on your feet emotionally, but remember that you and your spouse were divorced from each other, not from your children.

- If possible, work out a joint custody arrangement in which you and your ex-wife have equal responsibility for your children and time with them. Neither parent should be expected to assume all the economic or emotional responsibilities of child rearing. Joint custody isn't always possible, but more and more fathers and mothers are finding ways to make it work. It's best for the children, who get two involved parents. It's also best for the parents, who get to feel that they are both doing their fair share. Studies have found that quarter-time and half-time fathers usually feel better about themselves and their relationships with their children when they have regularly shared child-rearing responsibilities. [4]

- Even if you don't have joint custody and your time with your children is limited, make it clear to them that you will continue to love them and be closely involved in their lives. The idea of a father no longer being part of the family can be very frightening to a child. The best way to minimize such fears is for you to spend as much quality time as possible with your children on a regular basis. They will learn to expect you to be involved, be reassured by your availability, and be better able to deal with your comings and goings.

- Let your concern as a father help you get over any bitter feelings you may have toward your ex-wife. If you want to be an involved and effective father, you are probably going to have to work closely with her for many years as you both help your children cope with the effects of divorce.

- Don't become simply weekend entertainment for your children while their mother makes all the decisions in their lives. Making her responsible for everything may make her a target for your children's frustration and resentment, which will interfere with her effectiveness as a parent. Avoiding your responsibilities will also interfere with your effectiveness as a father, and your children deserve two good parents.

- Make the most of whatever time you have with your children and set an example of dependability, caring, and sensitivity. Your example can have lasting effects on many areas of their lives, including their love relationships and their ability to be good parents themselves.

- Try to have contact with your children at least every other day or so if only for a brief time. Keep up with what they are doing in school and with their friends. Call them regularly if you can't be there in person. Remain a part of their everyday life so that you really have things to share with one another. The frequency and regularity of your contacts is much more important than the fact that they last for several hours or include overnight visits. Too many fathers are overly concerned about the total number of hours they spend with their children instead of the quality of their involvement with them.

- Make stability an important factor in your custody arrangements. Family life and situations change, but it is extremely stressful when children are faced with a sudden loss of contact with one of their parents because either their mother or father has chosen to move to another area. A change in jobs or remarriage may force you or your ex-wife to move, but remember that great distance between parents usually creates problems for the children. In the case of young children, even one or two hours travel time can make easy access to both parents difficult. Before deciding to relocate, consider the importance of your children having two available and involved parents.

- Try to make custody arrangements in which your children seldom spend more than a few days at a time away from you or their mother. The split-custody routine in which children spend six months with each parent or the school year with one and vacations and holidays with the other usually interferes with family relationships and is likely to be quite upsetting to children, especially younger ones who lose the sense of continuity in a relationship if a parent is not around, even for a few days. In such situations, children often have difficulty developing a feeling of security in relationships with their parents and other family members.

- Live as close as possible to your ex-wife. It cuts down on transportation problems and can make life easier for everyone involved. Being close to your ex-wife may present problems if you and she are still having difficulties communicating, but remember that it is important for your children's sense of security to see their mother and father cooperate and share responsibility.

- Be careful how you talk about your children's mother in front of them. They need to love and respect both of their parents, and it can be very damaging for them to believe that either their mother or father is inadequate or worthless. It interferes with their own self-image and their ability to relate to other adults. When speaking to your children about their mother, try to emphasize that she and you are both good parents and that both of you are important parts of their lives.

STEPWORLD

We and our children now live in a world of stepfathers, -mothers, -brothers, -sisters, -cousins, and -grandparents. Nearly 5 million children live with a mother and stepfather. Another million live with a father and step-mother. One of four children born today will be part of a stepfamily by the time they are eighteen. For many of them this simply means gaining an extra family, but for others, step life means extra problems. They have to learn to deal with a new parent who isn't really their parent. They may have to learn to deal with stepbrothers and stepsisters, a different home and a different school. All of this can be difficult. Psychologist Mavis Hetherington, for example, finds that most children are hostile, sulking, negative, and angry during the early stages of remarriage. James Bray finds that they have more behavior problems than do children from intact families. And the most serious problems, according to both Hetherington and Bray, occur between daughters and stepfathers. Girls appear to be more stressed than boys by the new situation and have more family and social problems. One reason for this is that girls usually grow very close to their mothers during the single-parent period and often resent the intrusion of a man into a life they had shared with a single mother. Boys, on the other hand, are more likely to resent their mother for sending Dad away and are less likely than girls to resent the new man in the house.

Despite the fact that becoming a stepfather is likely to present such problems, Bray's long-term study indicates that with time and care most problems can be overcome. Five years after the remarriage, many of the boys in his study looked to their stepfathers for love and accepted their authority, and some of the girls were beginning to show signs of warming toward their stepfathers.[5]

- If you are a single father, do not get remarried simply because you want to find another mother for your children. Remember that not every woman will want to take on the responsibility of mothering your children. Find out how the potential stepmother feels about your children. Discuss your attitudes toward child rearing and work out a cooperative and realistic approach to family life.

- Remember that your children are likely to resent your new wife. She is taking their mother's place and is taking some of your time away from them. Discuss the possible problems with your children and their potential stepmother, and remember that bad feelings between them may lead to another divorce. The situation will be even more complicated if you and your new wife both have children from previous marriages. Time, patience, and acceptance of individual differences are crucial if the new family system is to be reasonably positive for everyone involved.

- Don't flaunt your love life in front of your children. It is hard enough for children of divorce to feel secure and make sense of their parents living apart. On the other hand, don't allow your children to manipulate you into sacrificing an important relationship. Assure them that your love for another woman will not interfere with your love for them and that caring and love are not restricted to only one type of relationship.

- If you do not have custody of your children, and your ex-wife is getting remarried, try to take a positive attitude toward the new stepfather. If both you and he are attached to the children, a type of shared and cooperative fatherhood is possible in which both of you feel comfortable nurturing the children.

- Do not let jealousy or your vanity get in the way of your children having an effective stepfather.

- Do not rush into stepfathering. It is difficult enough for two people to learn to live together, and it is more difficult when stepchildren are involved. It may take several months or more to even begin to work out a good relationship with your stepchildren.

- If you are about to become a stepfather, remember that you are entering an established family in which the natural father may still be involved and that your parenting efforts may meet with ambivalence from your new wife and resentment from her children and their father. Despite such barriers, your patience and positive involvement can have a constructive impact on the children. In some cases, children who were neglected by their fathers change from being unhappy and insecure to being self-assured and competent after a few years with a caring stepfather.

- Discuss what your potential wife expects of you as a stepfather. Does she expect you to stay in the background or gradually assume a cooperative parenting role? Be clear about this, and remember that the quality of your stepparenting will affect your relationship with both the children and their mother.

- Make sure you understand the relationships each of the natural parents has with the children. For example, do the children have an overidealized view of their father? This often happens in families where a father has died, and the stepfather finds himself trying to live up to the image of a saintly dead father. On the other hand, the children may be hostile and mistrustful toward a potential stepfather if their own father had badly mistreated them.

- You and your new stepchildren will both have to make many adjustments, but don't force the children to make too many changes too soon. It is probably best to keep a low profile and avoid unnecessary interference with the children at first.

- Keep changes to a minimum. Changes in life-style and

living arrangements can be very stressful, especially for children who will feel that they have no control over what is happening to their lives. If possible, move in with your new wife and her family instead of having them move in with you so they don't have to get used to a new home and a new school as well as a stepfather. If a young child has been sleeping in the same room with his or her mother, change the situation well in advance of your arrival on the scene. Try to avoid anything that forces an overnight change in the children's routines.

- Don't make extravagant promises or try to oversell the new family situation to the children. No matter how well intentioned, promises to take the children to every new movie or to cook their favorite meals every night will be virtually impossible to keep and will eventually undermine the children's trust in you.

- Try to be flexible and patient in allowing the family to adjust to you, but do not tolerate abusive behavior. The children must learn to respect your personal space, privacy, and property. Emotional closeness may not be possible at first, but mutual respect for each other's rights is crucial.

- Try to get close to your stepchildren, but do not insist that they treat you as if you were their father. Be available and accessible, but let them take the initiative. Be especially sensitive to the children's need for personal space.

- Don't try to force an unresponsive child to express affection by hugging and kissing. A stepfather who grabs, tickles, hugs, and kisses when there is not yet a basis for affection is likely to be rejected by the child. Young children may become attached to you rather easily, but older children and adolescents who are searching for their own identities and independence will probably find it difficult to accept you as a new parent or authority figure. In many cases, the most you can expect from an adolescent stepchild is a cordial but distant relationship.

■ Don't feel that you have to love your stepchildren or play a direct role as a parent instantly. But do work to develop an acceptance and tolerance of one another if you want to make the family work. This will take a great deal of time and patience on your part, but it will be worth the effort. Being a successful stepfather can be as rewarding as natural fatherhood.

REFERENCES

1. Meredith, D., "Dad and the Kids," *Psychology Today*, June 1985, p. 62.

2. Santrock, J., and Washak, R., "Father Custody and Social Development in Boys and Girls," *Journal of Social Issues*, Vol. 35, 1979, p. 112.

3. Wallerstein, J., and Blakeslee, S., *Second Chances: Men, Women and Children a Decade After Divorce*, New York: Ticknor and Fields, 1989.

4. Rosenthal, K., and Keshet, H., *Fathers Without Partners: A Study of Fathers and the Family After Marital Separation.* Totowa, NJ: Rowman & Littlefield, 1981.

5. Fischman, J., Stepdaughter Wars, *Psychology Today*, November 1988, p. 38.

SUGGESTED READINGS

HOW TO WIN AS A STEP FAMILY by Visher, E. and Visher, J., Bruner/Mazel, 1991.

GROWING UP WITH DIVORCE by Kalter, N., Fawcett, 1991.

THE CUSTODY REVOLUTION: THE FATHERHOOD FACTOR AND THE MOTHERHOOD MYSTIQUE by Warshak, R., Poseidon, 1992.

DIVORCE BUSTING: A REVOLUTIONARY AND RAPID PROGRAM FOR STAYING TOGETHER by Weiner-Davis, M., Summit Books, 1992.

Future Father

Things were falling apart, and John figured he must be having a midlife crisis. He'd spent twenty years in a less than satisfying job trying to earn a good living for his family, and now they all seemed to be abandoning him. His son had already gone off for college. His daughter would leave in a few weeks to travel for a year in India. His wife had devoted more and more time to her job as the kids grew older, and now she had been promoted and had even less time for home life. John felt deserted. His family had grown up and left him at home with an empty nest.

Ken didn't have the same experience. He'd worked long and hard to support his family and nurture his children, but he didn't feel deserted when they left home.

He still worried about them, but he was proud that they were finally making it on their own. He also felt relieved with no more tuition bills to pay! Ken's wife, like John's, was focusing more on her career, but Ken was proud of her accomplishments. And now that he didn't have to worry about tuition, he could afford to go on her business trips with her and do things they hadn't had the money or time to do before. Ken didn't feel like he had been left with an empty nest. He had his privacy back, a new feeling of independence, and a chance to establish an even closer relationship with his wife. Ken's midlife crisis passed almost unnoticed as he sat back and waited for his children to bring the next generation to visit the old family nest.

Is there such a thing as a midlife crisis? Yes, for some men. Psychologist Daniel J. Levinson and a number of other researchers have all found that many men, sometime between their late thirties and early fifties, experience a time of psychological and emotional turmoil as they begin to face changes in the way they feel about their jobs, their marriages, and their families. They begin to realize that they may not achieve the ambitious goals of their youth—they won't win the Pulitzer Prize, become the boss, or make a million. Their marriages may be on shaky ground, and their relationships with their increasingly independent children may have deteriorated.[1]

Even though many men do seem to experience a sort of crisis in midlife, as Levinson predicts, some psychologists are finding that the crisis may be related more to a social clock than to a biological clock. Psychologist Bernice Neugarten says the social environment greatly influences the timetable for when people expect to accomplish the major tasks of adult life, such as getting married, establishing a career, and having children.

People who do not accomplish these tasks on society's schedule, she says, are the ones most likely to find life stressful. Life events that occur on time, she says, usually are not stressful because they have been anticipated and prepared for. The empty nest syndrome, for instance, is not itself stressful for most middle-age parents. Instead, Neugarten says, it is when the children do not leave home at the appropriate time that stress occurs in both parents and children.[2]

Letting go of your children, however, is not easy. You've spent eighteen or so years living with and nurturing them, and now they want to leave you. But that, of course, is their job. They have to separate from you and establish themselves on the road to their own adulthood. Your job is to help them do just that without letting their independence destroy your relationship. This won't be easy for you—or for them. You can expect to feel a sense of loss, especially if you have been close to them, but you don't have to go into crisis. Instead, you should look forward to dealing with your children on a new basis— older adult to younger adult. If you continue to treat them like children, they will either fail to gain their own independence or will reject you altogether.

Instead of looking around and seeing an empty nest, you should look forward to a whole new phase of fatherhood. You may be free of day-to-day fathering duties, but your job is far from over. Once a father always a father and then, a grandfather.

To help you deal with this coming change in your life, you can do the following:

- Begin thinking about your children's eventual departure at least a year or two before it happens. Soften the blow by imagining what part you can now play in your children's adult lives. There will always be family reunions, and sooner or later you will be a grandfather. Think about what you have to learn from your children as their education and careers progress. Think about what you still have to teach them. You can be a counselor and advisor on career, family, and personal issues. You know a lot more than they do and still have a lot to offer. They are likely to appreciate your input if you treat them as adults but not if you treat them like children.

- Be prepared to deal with a certain amount of stress and anxiety when a son or daughter actually leaves home, especially if it is your youngest or only child. Your feelings are likely to be intense and to involve a sense of finality. Try to look back over the stages of your child's development and recognize that there has been a gradual growth toward independence. This is only another stage of development for both of you. Your love, care, and concern can continue, but each child must make his or her own way in the world. You should stay interested and supportive but do not think you can still control your adult children's destiny.

- Think back about how you finally separated from your parents. Was it an easy, gradual departure that you were completely prepared for, or was it a time of turmoil and hard feelings? Did you develop a more mature relationship with your parents, or do you still resent the way they tried to hold on to you? Keep your experiences and feelings in mind as you prepare to send your children down the road to adulthood.

- Develop your own interests and other relationships so that your children's departure does not leave a tremendous gap in your life, which is usually the case for parents whose only focus has been on their children. Mothers are more likely than fathers to suffer from the empty nest syndrome and become depressed when their children leave home because they usually have devoted more of their lives to parenting. But if you have been an equal partner in parenting, there is much less risk that your wife will feel at a loss when the children are gone.

- Don't be afraid that you are doomed to have a midlife crisis or suffer from the empty nest syndrome. Many men and women begin to feel a new sense of freedom once their children have left home. If you have moved successfully through your own adult development, you should be able to look forward to continued growth and an exciting future. Many men and women find that they are even happier in their marriages once their children have reached adulthood.

NURTURING NURTURANCE

Now that the nest is empty and your children are on the way to becoming independent and fulfilled adults, the next thing you can look forward to is seeing them become competent parents. And if you have been a competent father, your example is likely to be passed on to the next generation. If you have been a loving, involved father, your daughters will appreciate the importance of having a man involved in family matters and be prepared to share family and parenting responsibilities with their husbands. Your sons, too, will look forward with confidence to being fathers and will understand the importance of nurturance because they have experienced it themselves. They will be the kind of adults who know that they can be tender and loving as well as assertive and independent. They will understand that all these traits are important aspects of their personality and their own parenthood, and you will have the satisfaction of seeing them become caring and committed parents.

Some aspects of your new role might include the following . . .

- Set an example by also showing an interest in other children as well as your own, including those of relatives, neighbors, and friends. Invite them over to your house and take them on family outings. And don't simply treat them as entertainment for your kids. Talk to them. Get involved. Such caring does not have to be time-consuming, and it can be very gratifying for you and them.

- Pay special attention to children who live in mother-only families or whose fathers are not very involved with them. You'll be setting a good example and feel good about giving other children the kind of attention you had as a child or that you wish you had had more of. Just make sure that your interest in other children does not detract from one-on-one time with your children.

- In addition to setting an example, encourage your daughters and sons to be involved with younger children. Your sons and daughters can baby-sit for other families. They can work with organized programs for younger children or tutor or coach them informally. All such activities will help prepare them for their own parenthood.

- Be especially supportive of your sons' efforts to get involved with younger children since boys are more likely than girls to be teased by their friends for doing so.

- Encourage your children to learn about infant care, child development, and parenting before they become fathers or mothers (see Chapter 2). Even younger children should be taught about parenting and their future family responsibilities. You could even give your teen-agers a copy of *The Father Factor* to read.

THE GRANDFATHER FACTOR

Becoming a grandfather can be as exciting and as en-grossing as becoming a new father. It can draw you closer to your children and give you a sense of family connectedness. It can stir up memories of your own grandparents and help you realize that you are a genera-tional link to the future—an important aspect of coming to terms with your own mortality.

Being an involved grandfather can be a reenergizing experience and give your life new meaning, especially if you felt a sense of loss when your children went out on their own. Being a grandfather can be even easier and more fun than being a father. You can be close to and enjoy your grandchildren without the day-to-day respon-sibilities of being a father. You may not experience the intense identification you felt with your own young chil-dren but may be much freer to experience your grand-children as individuals. If you are retired or have at least eased off from the rat race, you may find that you have more time to spend with grandchildren than you did with your children. Many men even try to make up for ne-glecting their children by paying more attention to their grandchildren.

If you are a close and involved grandfather, you will have much to offer your grandchildren. Unfortunately, many men never get to discover the joys of grand-fathering. Some live too far away to develop close rela-tionships with their grandchildren. Others are still too preoccupied with their own problems to get involved. When psychiatrist Arthur Kornhaber interviewed more than 300 school age and adolescent children, he found that only about 5 percent had a very close and positive relationship with their grandparents.[3] These children described their grandparents in very positive terms, saying they were comfortable and at ease with them and that they felt that their grandparents were at the very center of their lives. And they gained from the experience. There was much more self-acceptance and feelings of specialness among them than among those who reported distant relationships with their grandparents. Those who were highly attached to their grandparents found it easy to relate to people of various ages. They felt at ease with elderly people and were less anxious about illness, aging, and issues related to death. Having positive attachments with grandparents as well as with parents broadened their ability to express sensitivity, empathy, compassion, and humor. In contrast, children who were not close to their grandparents felt greater discomfort with older people and more anxiety about illness and aging. They saw their grandparents in a negative way and tended to describe them as irascible, insensitive or intrusive. This was true even when the grandparents were quite generous with their money but not their time.

Perhaps the most dramatic example of the positive impact of grandfathers and men, in general, on the lives of children is seen in a study conducted by developmental researcher Norma Radin and her colleagues. They investigated grandparent-grandchild relationships in families in which unwed adolescent mothers were living with one or both of their parents. In these families, the grandchildren who had positively involved grandfathers were much more competent than those who had uninvolved or absent grandfathers. As infants, they were more responsive to and cooperative with their mothers; as one year olds, they showed less fear, anger, and distress; and as toddlers, they showed more cognitive maturity than did children with uninvolved grandfathers. These findings were especially strong in boys. It appears that the positive involvement of grandfathers in these families helped the teenage mothers to be more effective parents and contributed to the confidence and competence of their children.

Interestingly, Radin found no clear-cut evidence that grandmothers had a similar effect. This, she suggests, may be because a double dose of mothering does not make up for the lack of an involved father or grandfather.[4]

The benefits of grandfather–grandchild relationships are not restricted to the child. A major factor in psychological and physical well-being as you age will be a sense of closeness to your wife, siblings, children, and grandchildren. Many of the problems faced by older men, for example, are related to feelings of not being wanted or needed by younger family members. But a man who maintains close contact with the younger generations of his family is likely to have a support network to help him cope with loss and change as he grows older.

- If you are a father, remember that your parents and your wife's parents can be a great resource to you and your children—and not just as baby-sitters. Even if you don't want to spend a lot of time with your parents or in-laws, try to help your children develop close relationships with them. Your children will gain much from feeling close to a wide range of adults who have different perspectives.
- Don't force your children to spend time with their grandparents or pressure them to respond to each grandparent in the same way. Children should treat

others kindly, but it is unrealistic to expect them to love all family members in the same way. And remember that your respect for older family members sets an important example for your children.

- If you are a grandfather, try to develop a special relationship with your grandchildren for their good as well as your own. You can help them grow, and they can help you stay connected to your family. Your involvement can be especially helpful by providing an additional male presence if the children's father does not spend much time with them or if they live only with their mother.

- Take the initiative in getting involved with your grandchildren. Call them, write them, and most importantly, make time for face-to-face visits with them. Planning ahead for some time when you can be relaxed with them is likely to be much more mutually beneficial than simply seeing them when they need a baby-sitter. Do things with your grandchildren that you all enjoy, and share your skills and knowledge with them.

- When you are with your grandchildren, try to be supportive rather than critical of their parents. Do not be insensitive or interfere with your children's lives or their style of parenting. You can respect each other's separateness and still develop a close relationship with your grandchildren. The best way to do this is to make time for one-on-one activities with your grandchildren without the complication of other family relationships. An hour or two alone with a grandchild may be much more special than a whole day with him or her at a family gathering. Spending time alone with a grandchild will help provide a solid basis for your developing relationship. It may also help your children by giving them some time off from parenting.

- Don't feel that you have to treat all your grandchildren

the same or spend the same amount of time with each of them. Trying to dole out emotional investments this way may result in not having a close relationship with any grandchild. It is only natural for you to be more attached to some children than to others. Recognize and respect their differences and treat them accordingly.

LEGACY

"During early adulthood," says midlife researcher Daniel Levinson in *The Seasons of a Man's Life*, "a man may take special pleasure in begetting children and seeing them develop in variations of his own image. During middle adulthood, however, the satisfaction is of a somewhat different order. His offspring take their place in the adult world. He experiences their self-development and attainments as the fruits of his early adult labors. Their lives, their personal satisfactions, accomplishments and contributions are an essential part of his legacy. He will live on partly through them." But there is more to your legacy. You may leave your children a house and some money and an essential way of dealing with the world, but you also leave them the world they and their children will live in. And you begin to want that to be the best world possible. Levinson found that at midlife many men begin to show more concern for the well-being of their community and to feel responsible for the quality of life for succeeding generations. They become, in other words, social fathers.

Being a parent practically forces you to become a social father. It makes you think about the future. The potential effects, twenty or fifty years from now, of today's social and environmental policies seem much more dramatic when you think about the lives of your children and grandchildren. As a social father you feel a sense of responsibility that extends beyond your own family to include an active concern for the needs and welfare of the entire community. Social fathering can mean many things: leading a Boy Scout troop, coaching a Little League team, apprehending a purse snatcher, or demanding corporate accountability.

- Be an example to your children not only as an involved father but as a responsible citizen.
- Be a mentor to your own children as well as to other young adults. Offer them leadership, but don't treat them as children. Foster their growth and independence.
- Get involved with your local school system. By working with teachers and school administrators, you can have an important impact on children from other families as well as your own.
- Volunteer your time to groups that serve the needs of children. Big Brothers and other organizations that help provide meaningful relationships for needy children can be excellent outlets for social fatherhood. One of their major aims is to recruit volunteers committed to helping fatherless children.
- If you do get involved with a youth organization, do more than work as a coach or group leader. Your job as a social father requires that you give children individualized personal guidance. Many boys and girls have little opportunity for close relationships with caring adults, especially men.
- Do not, however, focus on contributions to the community at the expense of your own family. By serving others you can set a good example, but your first priority is to your family. If you neglect your children, you are being socially irresponsible in a very basic sense

even if you are aiding certain community, educational, or religious organizations. Being an effective parent and rearing your children to be responsible citizens is, in itself, one of the most important ways you can help your community.

REFERENCES

1. Levinson, D., *The Seasons of a Man's Life*. New York: Alfred A. Knopf, 1978.

2. Rosenfeld, A., and Stark, E., The Prime of Our Lives, *Psychology Today*, May 1987, p. 62.

3. Kornhaber, A., *Between Parents and Grandparents*. New York: Berkley Books, 1987.

4. Radin, N., Oyserman, D., and Benn, R., in Smith (Ed.) *The Psychology of Grandparenthood: An International Perspective*. London: Routledge, 1991.

SUGGESTED READINGS

FATHERS AND FAMILIES: PATERNAL FACTORS IN CHILD DEVELOPMENT by Biller, H., Auburn House, 1993.

WOMEN AND THEIR FATHERS: THE SEXUAL AND ROMANTIC IMPACT OF THE FIRST MAN IN YOUR LIFE by Secunda, V., Dell, 1992.

THE MEASURE OF A MAN: BECOMING THE FATHER YOU WISH YOUR FATHER HAD BEEN by Shapiro, J., Delacorte, 1993.

HOW FATHERS CARE FOR THE NEXT GENERATION: A FOUR-DECADE STUDY by Snarey, J., Harvard University Press, 1993.

Index